Always Looking Up

MADISON CLARK

ISBN: 978-1-4834-3326-4 (sc)
ISBN: 978-1-4834-3325-7 (e)

Library of Congress Control Number: 2015909780

Lulu Publishing Services rev. date: 7/8/2015

FOREWORD

*W*hen I think of which people in my life have taught me the most, Madi Clark is at the top of the list. What did I learn from her? I learned that despite the fact that almost every task in life poses a challenge; nothing is beyond accomplishing if you are determined.

I met Madi when she was a seventh grader; I was the counselor and physical education teacher. It was in my PE class where Madi taught me what sheer determination looked like. While I was trying to modify Madi's PE curriculum, she was determined to do what everyone else did. It looked something like this: One of the requirements while we were running track was to run the mile. I told Madi that if she ran a half-mile, I would give her full credit. Her response, "No thanks, Mrs. De Jong. I want to run the whole mile." And, she did! Then when we were playing basketball, I told Madi that if she completed all the drills to the best of her ability, I wouldn't require her to make a basket. Her response, "No thanks, Mrs. De Jong. I'm going to make a basket if that's okay with you." And ... she did!

Determination defines Madi because life would look very different if she didn't have it. Life would sort of live around Madi, but that's not the life that Madi wants, so it's not the one she settles for. When Madi came to school, her parents sent a letter explaining exactly what achondroplasia/ dwarfism, or being a little person, was and what Madi's limitations were.

Right after this, there was a sentence in the letter that said, "We are raising Madi to do things for herself because we want her to grow up to be an independent adult. So, if she says she wants to try something herself, please let her. That's our request."

Madi Clark is a little person, and she has many limitations because of her condition, but she is also one of the strongest people I know. My hope as you read the pages of her book is that you get to know the Madi I know: one of the most determined individuals on the planet and someone who can help us all learn to see people with limitations for who they are and what they can do. I'm so proud of Madi for sharing her story here and I trust that when you've finished reading it, you'll have a much better understanding of dwarfism and hopefully a better idea of how to celebrate and respect people like Madi.

With much love
Bonnie De Jong

DEDICATION

This book is dedicated to my lovely parents, Rob and Leanne. Without the two of you, I wouldn't be the person I am now. Both of you have given me the confidence I have needed to tackle my biggest challenges. I am proud to be your daughter and admire the love you share for one another.

And to my protectors (aka brothers and sister-in-law), Brad, Molly, Mitchell, and Miles; you all have always looked out for me over the years and have given me the privilege of being an auntie to Kirra, Gavin, and Vincent.

And for everyone who has ever been teased, laughed at, ridiculed, or bullied, this book is dedicated to you for being so strong.

Lastly, this book is in memory of my great-grandmother, GG, and my weekend dad, Tom LeBrun; I love and miss you both dearly.

XO Madi

CONTENTS

INTRODUCTION

The greatest story you will ever tell is your own.

—Charlie Rose

I am an ordinary girl living an almost ordinary life. Though different from the majority, my life is mine, and I've learned to embrace it. Is it an easy life? Absolutely not. As you will learn from reading my story, it comes with physical and emotional challenges, and many adjustments. It has not been an easy life, and I have often sat with my head in my hands and asked, "Why me?"

Each day consists of something new, but most days, my schedule usually looks like this:

6:15 a.m.: My alarm tells me it is time to start my day! I don't want to get up, so I lie there half-awake, close to going back to sleep.

6:30 a.m.: I finally get the energy to climb out of bed. Not a big fan of morning breath (mine or anyone else's), so I start my day by brushing my teeth.

6:45 a.m.: I get dressed, put on my makeup, and do my hair. Most nights I will sleep with my hair in a braid so that in the morning, all I have to do is take the braid out because my hair is perfectly wavy—my favorite look.

7:00 a.m.: I usually have a little bit of time to clean my house, which consists of taking out the bathroom trash, emptying the dishwasher (assuming I remembered to run it the night before), tidying up the kitchen and bathroom, and, on some days, vacuuming the carpets and tile floor in every room.

7:30 a.m.: I rush out of the house and into my car because it is time to get to school.

1:00 p.m.: Classes have ended, and I'm heading back home or to any appointments that I have scheduled that day.

2:00 p.m.: I then study and complete any homework that is due the next day or the following week.

3:15 p.m.: I head to the gym, which is one of my all-time favorite places, to work out.

5:00 p.m.: I head home to shower and finish the rest of my homework.

6:30 p.m.: The family and I sit down to have dinner.

8:00 p.m.: I watch a few of my favorite TV shows or catch up with a friend over the phone or Skype.

11:00 p.m.: The day is done, gone the sun, good night and sweet dreams.

While I lie in bed and go to sleep, I dream of a girl with longer arms and legs. I dream of a girl being accepted kindly by all who meet her for not only who she is inside, but also for what she looks like on the outside. This girl that I dream of, I dream that she is me.

I believe that once people get to know me, they do ultimately accept me. I know through experience that at first glance, my appearance is met with laughter and mockery and standoffishness. When I wake up and look in the mirror, I accept the reality that my dream of having longer arms and legs will never be. I accept what I see in that mirror as my reality. If I pinched myself, I would still be standing there looking at that same girl, in that same body.

Thankfully, with each day's challenges, I have people who are always there to hold my hand. If it weren't for those wonderfully supportive people and the people who have been encouraging me throughout my life, I'm not sure how I would go on day by day. My friends, family, and support system have all helped me to become the strong and confident person that I am today.

People come into your life for a reason and a purpose that you may never fully know, but God always does. Each person you meet, even if it is just a little glance in your direction while walking down the street, is someone who may somehow make a difference in your life. Never take any interaction for granted because you may not instantly be aware how that chance meeting may ultimately alter your life.

I never thought I would write a book about my life, and neither did my family or friends. To be honest, I didn't consider writing a book until I was in high school. It was then that I began to feel I had a story to tell to others, a story that may have a positive impact on not only people of little stature, but any person who has challenges to conquer and has questioned whether it is sometimes just easier to give up. When I came to the realization that I may indeed have a story to tell, I just began writing. I poured out everything that was inside me and shared all of the thoughts I had been holding back. Some days, the words flowed easier than others and the memories of my life poured from my soul, while other days, I struggled to get into that creative rhythm.

Through this process of collecting thoughts, I often questioned why I think I am unique or special enough to have a memoir that other people may care to read. I also was not quite sure if I was ready to share with the world the challenges that I face on a daily basis or how I am able to overcome them. I was uncertain if this would just become one of those *projects* that I would not see through to completion. However, I realize that if I want to make an impact on the world, to make the world a brighter place with more color and inspiration, then it is my responsibility, my obligation, to share my story with those I may potentially impact in a positive manner. Writing about my challenges may be a way to touch others and really speak to them. I hope that this book will encourage and motivate others to stay strong, to follow their heart, and to be that person they are destined to be.

CHAPTER 1

Let's Start at the Beginning

As I begin to write this, I am twenty-one years old and only five stair steps high, which is the height of an average six-year-old child. The top of my head reaches to the hips of an average person. I am four feet, one inch, and this is as tall as I am going to be for the rest of my life. Stop for a moment and envision what life is like as an adult at this height. I can't reach the drinking fountain. I need help selecting any item higher than the second shelf at the grocery store, and I can't take any item off the top shelf of the refrigerator. I need accommodations in my car when I drive, I have to have my clothes altered, I am towered over by the typical fourth grader, and I can barely be seen if I stand up to a bar to order myself a glass of wine.

Neither my parents nor the doctors had any warning that a baby girl with a type of dwarfism called achondroplasia would be coming into the world on that beautiful spring morning of April 14, 1993. When my parents got married, they knew they wanted to have children, but never in their wildest dreams did they imagine giving birth to a baby with dwarfism. To be honest, they had no clue what dwarfism was until my mom was pregnant with me and learned that not all was well as her pregnancy neared full term.

My momma pregnant with me

On March 15, 1993, Mom was nearly eight months pregnant and went to her obstetrician for a routine ultrasound. As she was lying on the table hoping to see images of her soon-to-be baby girl, the technician unexpectedly stopped the procedure and said something was wrong with the machine. He advised my mom that she would need to have another ultrasound performed at the hospital as soon as it could be rescheduled. Disappointed, but suspecting it was nothing to be concerned about, Mom underwent the same procedure two days later at Long Beach Memorial. To her utter shock, the doctor explained that my arms and legs measured a lot shorter than they were supposed to be at that point in my gestational growth. Doctors warned my parents that I may have either achondroplasia or Down syndrome, but they thought that it was more likely achondroplasia. The gene for achondroplasia had not yet been discovered at that time, but the doctors knew the gene for Down syndrome so they recommended my mom have an amniocentesis to either confirm or rule out Down syndrome. To everyone's surprise, the results came back on March 23, my mom's birthday.

The test ruled out Down syndrome, and my parents learned that I would most likely be born with achondroplasia, a type of dwarfism that, up to the week before, they had known little or nothing about. What they instantly accepted was that life would change forever for their family, and though it didn't scare them, they knew adjustments would have to be made. I was born three weeks later, which was two weeks early.

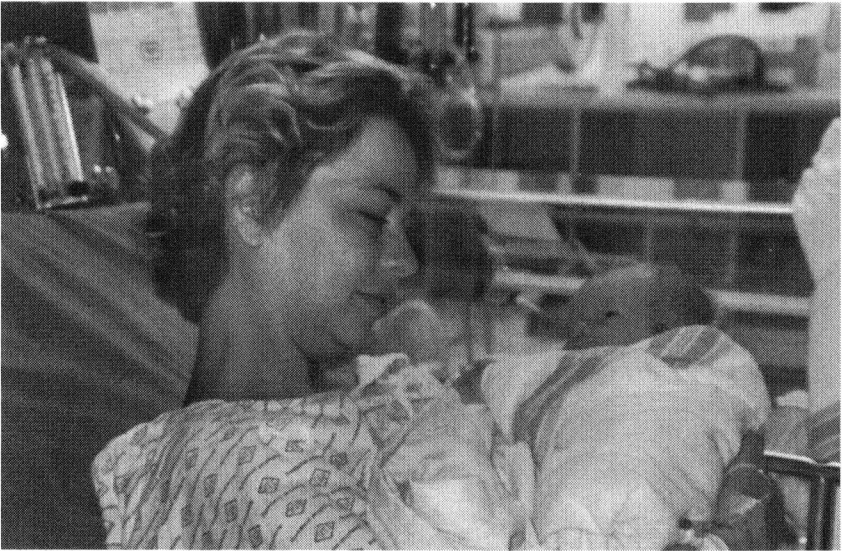

April 14, 1993
I was born...

Here are some interesting facts regarding the statistical anomaly of being born with dwarfism. The odds are one in every ten thousand that two average-sized parents with no genetic history of dwarfism will give birth to a little person. This means the odds of my existence as we know it are about .0001 percent. I'm not a numbers person, but I know as small as I am physically, that percentage is a whole lot smaller. I was one of those chosen statistical aberrations. I was picked by God to forever stand out from everyone around me. That is the true definition of incredible: one of God's chosen few.

Dwarfism is a condition characterized by short stature. Generally, it is defined as an adult who is four feet, ten inches or shorter. The average adult height of a person with dwarfism is four feet. So how is it that I was born of short stature into a family full of very tall individuals? Well, let me tell you. Over 80 percent of all people born with dwarfism have average-height parents. My type of dwarfism, achondroplasia, is the most common type and occurs in one out of every twenty-five thousand to forty thousand births. In my case, achondroplasia was caused by a spontaneous genetic mutation in either the egg or sperm and was not from either parent's genetic makeup.

In general, those with dwarfism are divided into two broad categories: proportionate dwarfism and disproportionate dwarfism. Proportionate dwarfism is usually caused by a growth-hormone deficiency that limits overall growth and development. The limbs, trunk, and head are all small and in proportion to each other. Disproportionate dwarfism results in some parts of the body being small while others are of average size or above-average size.

Achondroplasia (short-limbed dwarfism), or *achon* for short, is a type of disproportionate dwarfism. The word *achondroplasia* simply means "without cartilage formation." In those with achondroplasia, the long bones don't develop typically, making the arms and legs disproportionately short and sometimes curved. Characteristics of people with achondroplasia include an average-size trunk; short arms and legs; extremely short upper arms and thighs; short fingers, often with a wide separation between the middle and ring fingers; limited range of motion at the elbows; a prominent forehead; a flattened bridge of the nose; and an adult height of around four feet. When some people see a person with dwarfism, they assume that it's a disease that requires a cure. They often think it is accompanied by intellectual disability. In both cases, this isn't accurate. Dwarfism is a rare genetic mutation, not a disease, and in the large majority of cases, the individual is still a regular, fully capable human being with the same amount of intelligence as any average-size person.

My 2 year old self pretending to be a cowgirl while eating popcorn.

People who are of short stature can become parents, but the odds of giving birth to a short-statured child vary with each diagnosis. A person with achondroplasia, for example, has one dwarfism gene and one "average-size" gene. If both parents have achondroplasia, there is a 25 percent chance that their child will inherit the nondwarfism gene from each parent and be of average size. There is a 50 percent chance the child will inherit one dwarfism gene and one nondwarfism gene and thus will have achondroplasia, just like their parents. Lastly, there is a 25 percent chance that the child will inherit both dwarfism genes, a condition known as double dominance, which always ends in death at birth or shortly thereafter.

Once my parents found out that their baby girl would be born with dwarfism, they began researching and becoming educated about everything one should ever need to know about it. When I finally made my grand appearance, we, as a family, joined an organization called Little People of America (LPA). We began networking through online connections and even attended meetings with an entire community of families raising children with dwarfism across the United States. So right from the start, I grew up with people who were just like me.

From the very day I was born, I faced life accompanied by a label. Applying a label in today's society is never okay, but we tend to do it all the time. People are fat, skinny, white, black, rich, poor, stupid, smart, and on and on. We are a society that more often than not feels the need to characterize people. If one is to attach a label to me, it would be *little person, person of short stature,* or *dwarf,* but the term *midget, munchkin,* or any other politically or socially unacceptable term should not be used. *Little person* is okay because I am literally little and a person. I am referred to as *the little person* if one doesn't recall or remember my name. "You know the little person?" or "The little person just walked past me!"

It's quite obvious to whom they are referring when someone says, "the little person," since I am the one and only in my immediate world. I take no offense to this phrase and use it most often when describing my friends who are of similar stature. For short, we say LP, and when describing people who are average height, we say AP (average person). *Little person* and *person of short stature* are currently preferred terms. It's also acceptable if one calls me a dwarf. Keep in mind I am not Sneezy, Bashful, Happy, Doc, Dopey, or Sleepy, though like everyone, I can occasionally be Grumpy. Though *dwarf* is defined by the dictionary as "a person of usually small stature whose body proportions are abnormal," there is also a definition that says, "A small, legendary, man-like being who is usually misshapen and ugly and skilled as a craftsman." Calling me a dwarf isn't at all bad, but I don't see or classify myself as an ugly and misshapen craftsman.

Sitting up all by myself.

My medical record describes me as an achondroplastic dwarf. That word will follow me until the day I die. *Midget,* however, is a word considered offensive by most people of short stature. The term dates back to 1865, when it was used at circus freak shows and applied only to short-statured people who were displayed for public amusement. The word will forever have the power to make me feel worthless and incredibly ugly. It hurts to hear that word uttered from someone's mouth or from the television. When one asks why *midget* is so offensive, I simply say, "It's like calling an African-American person the *n* word." Not many people know this, but everyone should know how offensive the word can be.

The best thing you could ever possibly call me is my actual name. Until I can be Madison the girlfriend, fiancée, wife, college graduate, mother, speech therapist, and grandma, I am Madison the granddaughter, daughter, sister, aunt, niece, cousin, friend, neighbor, nanny, and now, author. Wahoo!

Everyone has the power to change ignorance and labels. Therefore, I promise with everything I have inside of me to do my part to help eliminate the negative labels that people put on others.

CHAPTER 2

Picture Snapping, Laughter, and All the Stares

*I*t is a rare day when people that I encounter do not stare or take pictures of me. It's hard to believe that people can be so bold, I know, but it's the truth. Nothing is more humiliating than being laughed at, ridiculed, or made the subject of someone else's jokes. It's easy for people who are not considered different to insist that I'm exaggerating or over-dramatizing, but it is the truth. Friends have said to me, "You must not go a day in your life without someone looking at you differently!" I'm afraid they are right. There is never such a day for me. Every day, I am on the public stage, being stared or gawked at like I am a circus side show.

Perfect strangers often have no problem approaching me and asking for a picture as if I am some sort of freak. Usually, they want to put the photo up on the Internet or on social media sites, like Facebook, Twitter, or Instagram, to show others that they have spotted a *midget*. Needless to say, this is humiliating, as well as ignorant, on their behalf.

There was a time when I was thrilled that someone would want to take a picture of me. I felt like I was unique in my own little way. As I got older, however, I became conscious of the fact that they were mocking me and not simply happy to meet me. I knew that this needed to be stopped. It is rude to take pictures of a person just because they look different. I catch people taking pictures of me wherever I go. It frequently happens at a mall or even at the "happiest place on earth," Disneyland, where I visit rather often, being a California girl. I cannot do anything except to ask nicely for the person taking the picture to please stop. I don't want to be rude, but it sometimes comes to that. Twice, I've found my own photo on Instagram shortly after it had been taken. Discovering this caused me much pain and humiliation.

On one occasion that I will never forget, I went out to run an errand for my dad. He asked me to go to the bank for him to deposit a check. I really wasn't in the mood to go, because I was busy doing my own thing and the thought of stopping at the bank didn't sound fun. Whether I wanted to go or not, I knew I had to, so I hopped in my car and headed out. I got into the left lane to turn into the parking lot and waited for all the cars to pass going the opposite direction. As I was getting ready to turn, I saw a man in a white truck stopped in the lane to the right of me. Since there was no traffic in front of him, there really wasn't any reason for him to stop. I looked over at him, and I realized what he was doing. He had his camera phone pointed straight at me, trying to capture a picture. When he saw me looking at him, he had the nerve to laugh and drive away. There I was, sitting in the left-hand turn lane, completely shocked. I was disgusted and humiliated that someone could be that uncaring about another human being's feelings. I went numb—once again the butt of someone's warped sense of humor.

All of my life I have been told that I need to learn how to stick up for myself. I need to tell people how I'm feeling and not keep things inside for fear of upsetting them. I was frequently asked questions like, "Did you defend yourself?" "Did you take a picture of them?" "Did you ask them to delete it?" When this happened, I instantly heard a lifetime of voices and foolishly decided to go after the picture-snapping guy in the truck, who by this time was already at the end of the street. After turning down several side streets trying to catch up, I was stopped by a red light. By this time, he was out of my sight, and it was likely just as well. I calmed down a bit and realized that I should just turn around and go back to the bank. I sensed that if he was dumb enough to take a picture of me, then he would more than likely also be dumb enough to post it on Instagram under the hashtag *#midget.*

After getting home and telling my dad the story, I searched #midget on Instagram, and sure enough, there was my image. I thought that I would cry when I saw it, but I simply couldn't. After finding the picture, I studied his profile, figured out his name, and found him on Facebook. I couldn't stop there and creeped on him long enough to learn that he had a girlfriend. My dad sent his girlfriend a private message letting her know what her boyfriend had done. My dad encouraged me to tell my oldest brother, Brad, to comment on the picture and tell him to take it off. I took a screenshot of the picture on my iPhone and sent it to Brad, letting him know where I had found it. It took Brad only a minute to write to this man, telling him that he needed to take the picture down. Several friends of mine, as well as, my youngest brother, got involved, and it instantly took over Facebook. A couple of my mom's friends said that they were friends with this guy's parents and asked if we wanted their number. Another friend called the guy himself and had a chat with him. I really just wanted an apology. I wanted him to meet me in person to give me a sincere apology first-hand.

The next day my house phone rang, but no one was home to answer it. Upon our return home, we listened to the voice mail, and it was actually the man telling me that he was sorry about what he had done and that he didn't mean to post it on Instagram. Wait, what? Did I hear that right? He didn't mean to post my photo on Instagram with the hashtag #midget? The reality was that he just didn't mean for me to find it. This is just one of the many incidents that I have been subjected to. It's sad to say, but this is the price I have to pay to living in a world where I'm considered different from the norm.

When someone approaches me and asks if they can take a picture, often I just say no. To me, however, there is a difference between secretly snapping a photo while driving by and seeing me on a street, stopping to say hi, and eventually asking if it's all right to take a picture together. If I feel like that the person might be too obsessed with little people or if they want a picture because they want to make fun of me, then I'll politely tell them no. I rarely meet anyone who asks for a picture that doesn't have some sort of LP fetish or intentions that won't be harmful to me.

Some people think that little people are rude and that we don't want others to say hello or even ask a question. Just like anyone else, some of us are friendly and some are not. I think part of this is a negative stereotype from TV and the movies.

I love meeting new people and have no issue answering most questions they may have. I'd prefer that people ask a question in order to become educated than not ask, assume things, and walk around ignorant later. One shouldn't make assumptions about people or their challenges. If you have a question surrounding the life of a little person, simply ask it. That person's answers should be your first and best resource. The one thing that most people should understand about people who are in a wheelchair, who are short, blind, or have no arms or legs, is that they are people too. As I stated earlier, different does not indicate less human or a freak; it simply indicates different. Some people really appreciate the opportunity to talk about their disability and to educate others about differences or accessibility issues, and others don't like to talk about these things at all. What is important is that you respect the person and see them beyond their disability or what they may look like.

People look at me or take pictures, not because I am on a reality TV show or because I am the most gorgeous female that they have ever laid eyes on, but instead because I am short. It makes me wish that they would see me for who I really am.

Another occurrence that I encounter on a daily basis would be children who stare at me until a parent has the wherewithal to turn the child's head around or their eyes grow tired. When children stare, I ultimately smile and give them a look that means *I can see you, and you should stop.* They walk a little, then turn, look back, and usually keep on staring. Unfortunately, it's not just little kids that stare, but often adults as well. I mostly catch the young kids' eyes more often because I am the same height as they are. I think younger kids look at me because they do not know what is and isn't rude. I don't often encounter teenagers who stare, maybe because they have learned that it's not polite.

At times, I confuse people because they will mistake me for a child until I turn around and they see that my features are adult. It's funny to see their faces because their expressions instantly change. They look and look again because they thought I was just a little kid.

People do not really understand how much others stare until they go someplace in public with me and witness it for themselves. One of the first times I went to the mall with my good friend from high school, we walked through the double doors and continued to the food court. We got to the end of the food court when she asked, "Who are all these people staring at?"

I couldn't hold back a little chuckle and said, "They are looking at me."

Another time when my family and I took a high school friend, Brooke, to my family's favorite campground, some kids there were staring at me. When we walked away, I could hear them laughing, and it was obvious that they were laughing at me. Brooke looked down at me and said, "I'm sorry. I'm sorry you have to go through this."

I told her, "I'm used to it," and I laughed it off, but deep down I wasn't and never will get used to it at all.

It can be upsetting at times when I am out in public with my dad and kids stare because he will give them a terrifying look, like he's going to attack them or something. I feel bad for the kids when my dad does that, and I end up yelling at him to stop. One time when I was twelve, I walked out of a restaurant when my family and I were waiting to be seated. A couple kids were laughing, and my dad got too uptight and I couldn't handle it. I felt like I was stuck in the middle. It is hard for my dad to watch people stare at his daughter, and I totally understand, but him giving kids those stares makes me feel extremely awkward. I always seem to know when someone will stare, and I hope and pray that by the time they realize I am little, I am out the door and don't have to deal with it. It can be hard at times to think that I confuse people who know nothing about dwarfism. Is it my fault that I go out in public and make people confused? I could sit in my house every day, for the rest of my life, and not participate with the outside world; but I don't choose to do that. I don't choose to do that because that would get really boring, and this is a positive way for me to educate individuals about dwarfism and about anyone who may look different. I don't want to feel sorry for myself or have someone else feel sorry for me, so I would rather go out in the world and face a little teasing than sit in my house, cry, complain, and let life pass me by.

People frequently stop and ask how old I am, though when I was younger, I was rarely asked. Instead, they would either ask whoever I was with as if I wasn't old enough or intelligent enough to answer the question. Being made to feel invisible because you are different is also very unsettling. When I was out in public with my mom or dad and somebody asked how old I was, my parents would always reply, "Ask her; she can talk." Whenever my mom told a little boy or girl that, their eyes became bigger, and they usually ran away. Their frightened response not only confused and angered me, it mostly saddened me. Now, when children ask me, I absolutely love it and accept that they are just curious; I was the same way when I was their age.

In the future, if someone asks my parents if I can talk, or asks how old I am, I will hold out my hand and say, "Hi, my name is Madi. What's yours?" I don't want to be some alien that came down from outer space, but it sure feels like it sometimes.

I've also had my small stature work the opposite way at times when people assumed I was older than I was. That was good at times, but it can get me in a little trouble. At Aunt Mimi's wedding, I was handed a glass of champagne because they figured that I was old enough to drink. Keep in mind that at the time, I was only twelve and didn't even knew what makeup was, let alone a glass of champagne. When my aunt got married, she asked me to be one of her bridesmaids, and I happily accepted the invitation. It turned out that her wedding in Santa Barbara was on the same weekend that my brother had a baseball tournament, so my grandpa and his wife took me to the wedding while my parents spent the weekend with my brother. During the reception dinner, Aunt Dawn sat right next to me. When I was handed the glass of champagne, both of us looked at each other and laughed. I laughed because I couldn't believe that I was being allowed to drink and my parents weren't there to participate in the moment. Aunt Dawn laughed because she knew I was way too young to drink and, without any hesitation, took the glass away from me and sat it in front of her plate. It was worth a try at least. So there it is—seems like I'm caught in the middle and never judged as my actual age.

CHAPTER 3

Adapting to the World around Me

*L*iving in a world that is not made for me is tough, but I have made adaptations to get over the hurdles and am still able to live the easiest way possible. My dwarfism is never a reason why I cannot do something; it's really become a reason why I should give it a valiant try. I have learned, through trial and error, how to accommodate just about any situation that I am presented with. Being a little person, there are some challenges that I face that are different from those of average height people, such as reaching things that are up high, finding clothes that fit, driving a car, and getting accepted for a job.

Reaching things that are high can sometimes seem impossible if I don't have a stool, a way to climb up shelves, or someone who's close by so I can ask for assistance. In certain situations, simply asking for someone's help to get something off the top shelf may be the fastest way to accomplish a simple task, but I don't find it the most gratifying. If I count on others each time I need something, then I'm not really taking responsibility for my own life. I'm relying on others to do things for me when I'm trying to prove to society that I'm actually capable of doing things for myself. If there were no one around to help me reach the pasta sauce, for example, then I certainly can't blame them when I don't have dinner that night. How I react to any situation I'm presented with is entirely up to me, and I am ultimately responsible for the outcome. Climbing on shelves might not be the safest way to get something down (especially after having neck surgery), but sometimes it's the most convenient way at that time. Climbing on shelves usually only happens when there is no stool in sight. I have a stool in every room of my house and in every car my family owns to make things more convenient. I may not always rely on others to help me out, but I certainly rely on a stool.

When I travel, I always make room in my suitcase for my black fold-up stool because I never know when I will need it. When I visit family and close friends at their homes, there's usually a stool there waiting for me. From time to time, family friends will ask me to house sit while they are away on vacation, and it's nice when I can usually find stools around the house for me to use.

I am frequently asked where I buy my clothes. Finding outfits that fit me can be tough at times, especially pants, dresses, or jackets. For the most part, the majority of the pants I buy have to be altered, aside for a few that were meant to be capris for someone tall. I shop for most of my clothes where any other young women shop: Forever 21, Tilly's, Pac Sun, Nordstrom, and Target. To be honest, if I walk into a random shop and find something cute that fits great, then I'll buy it. I am frequently asked why I don't shop in the kids section so I don't have the problem of having to alter my clothes. My butt and hips are the size of or even bigger than most women, so I often can't fit even one leg in little girl's pants without getting stuck.

When most people go into a store to buy a pair of pants, they probably don't ever think about having to make alterations because things fit just fine. When little people (or anyone who is just short) go into a store to buy pants, the thought of altering them is already established in our heads before we enter the store. It is hard to buy pants that fit perfectly in the hips and butt and yet are short enough to wear without having to spend more on alternations. Hemming my clothes can be pricy. When I was younger, my grandma would

17

alter my clothes for me, but living thirty minutes away from each other never made it easy. She still alters things for me occasionally, but I usually go to a local cleaners a couple minutes from my house, or a new place that was recommended to us by a friend who is also a little person.

Finding clothes that fit is one thing, but finding furniture is another. My legs dangle from every chair I sit in, and I have to jump to get up on any bed. For every countertop, toilet, and bookshelf I try to ascend, I have to use a stool. When I move out and get my own place, I would love to have furniture that is easy for me to get on and off of. I'd like a chair that I can sit on and still have my feet touch the floor. Even though I would love to have furniture to fit me or counters low enough to cook on, I also want them to be of average height for my friends and family when they come over. I want them to feel at home too. I can't wait to move out and be able to find my own furniture that will make everyone who comes into my home feel comfortable.

In the past, I have had friends tell me that I can't do something because my legs are too short. They've said, "I won't invite her, because she won't be able to keep up with us." I've heard all kinds of things like that, and truthfully, that's my reason for being: to show people that I can do anything and everything even if my legs are half their size. I can still run or walk a 10K, which I have done. I can be a doctor or a teacher, or even become a mom. I can be whatever I want to be if I just put my heart and mind to it. Right now, little people aren't quite accepted in society, but I hope that this will ultimately change.

A driver's license is something that most children look forward to getting when they are in high school. It was something I looked forward to, but I wasn't sure how I would accomplish that. If you are wondering if I can drive, well yes, I can. How do I do it? I do it with a wonderful accommodation called pedal extensions. My dad says they are the greatest invention out there. Without them, there would not be a way for me to jump in my car and drive off on my own. I would have to count on everybody else to take me places for the rest of my life, and I don't want to do that. I want to be independent and do things on my own. Before I got my own car, my dad put my pedal extensions on his car each time I needed to drive. They usually took him about five to ten minutes to put on, so not too bad. They require some tools to take on and off, and you have to have a strong back to reach down where the pedals are to hook them on top. Then, you have to screw them on from the back of the pedal. I have heard stories of people who had their gas or brake pedal fall off while they were driving. They had to reach all the way down where the actual pedal is with their foot, barely seeing out the window, to be able to pull off to the side of the road. If that were to ever happen to me, I don't know what I would do. That is really scary for me to think about.

I also have a handicapped-parking placard, which at times is my life saver. Most people think the main reason I have one is because my legs are short and I walk slow, but that's not the case. Parking close to stores, buildings, and restaurants saves time and knee pain, but being only the height of a child puts me out of sight of just about anyone backing up their car. Most drivers are not thinking to look for a really short girl, and unless they have a backup camera, I can easily be missed. The farther I park from a building, the more cars I have to walk behind, and the more opportunities there are for me to get run over. I will use that little blue handicap placard wherever I go because I don't want to take a chance of being hit by a car.

Finding a job isn't always easy in today's society regardless of height, but being of short stature or having a disability can make it a lot harder. Not every company will accept the fact that I may need a stool to stand on to fold an item of clothing or to blend a drink. Do I think it's fair? Absolutely not. What can I do about it? Try to prove them wrong. When I go to apply for a job, I ask to speak with the manager. I am often told no the moment the manager looks my way. It's biased without getting to know a person and what they may be able to bring to a company. How can a manager decide on the basis of your looks? To avoid this harsh reality of life and the fact that little people are often turned down after a job interview, many are willing to dress up in costumes or take part in films in which little people are entertainers and are ridiculed for their physical appearance. I find it sad that many people's only exposure to a person of short stature has to be one dressed up in a costume or being thrown from across the room (also known as dwarf-tossing). I find it sad that filmmakers allow it, and little people feel that they have to take roles such as these. I know of a few films that have done a disservice to little people with regards to how LPs are viewed in society. On the other hand, I know of a few television shows, such as *The Little Couple* and *Little People, Big World*, that do an amazing job portraying LPs as real people.

Although my parents make sure I am provided with everything I need to be successful, they have *never* let me use my short stature as an excuse. No step stool? That's okay. I'll climb my way up. Didn't get hired for a job? It's cool. There's something bigger in store for me in the future. I can't find clothes that are short enough to wear the same day I buy them? I just have to get them altered. It may not always be easy, but I take pride in the fact that I am able to adjust to certain things that were not meant for me. I truly believe this ability extends to all aspects of my life, on both physical and emotional levels.

CHAPTER 4

Family

*F*amily means *everything* to me. My family allows me to be myself and accepts me for who I am. We love and care for one another, and (try to) support each other through thick and thin. Family means nobody gets left behind. They may not agree with you all the time, but they love you. That is my family!

Love my family

I love my family, all nine members: my parents, Rob and Leanne; my three brothers, Brad, Mitch, and Dewey; my sister-in-law Molly; my niece Kirra; and my nephews, Gavin and Vincent. They are all unique in their own way, and they've let me know that if I fall, they will surely help me up … if not with a helping hand, then with words of encouragement. My parents do a wonderful job of making sure that we are all loved, cared for, and hopefully happy. They both provide a place for us that we can go to if we need advice, a hand to hold, or to feel connected again. That place is what I call my home. Home is where I go if I need a break from the real world—always welcoming, always safe. Home is a judgment-free zone where my parents raised Mitch, Dewey, and me.

Love being their auntie! Gavin, Vincent, and Kirra

My parents are the greatest. They go out of their way to not only make my family happy, but to also open their doors for everyone else with whom they come into contact. They want us to achieve all of our goals in life, and they push us to become better individuals. My mom is my role model. She's a leader, a giver, a provider, and the nicest and most caring woman you will ever meet. She's nurturing, affectionate, and the greatest cook. My dad is also a provider and a hard worker. He's dedicated to his family and work, honest, loving, and a cancer survivor.

I love my mom, and I would do anything for her. The times we spend together are wonderful and very important to me. I can talk to her about anything and everything, and I know that she will always listen and always have good advice. She is the greatest influence in my life, not only as a mom, but also as a friend. When she was in high school, she would drive all over town with her friends in her Fiat, with the top down and surfboards coming out of the back, pretending to be surfers. No longer a poser, she now either sits on the sand and takes pictures of my brothers and me and my dad surfing, or reads a book or magazine at the beach. To this day, when my mom is around her friends from high school, they automatically start telling stories about when they went to Neff High School together. It is neat to see because I always think, *Wow, this is going to be me and my friends when we are all grown up and have families of our own. We will get together and talk about our high school memories from Valley Christian.* She is a great mother, wife, sister, grandma, friend, and aunt.

She is also known as the cleaner, the person who makes her kids get down on their hands and knees and scrub the floor. That's not really the truth, but one of her friends jokes around with her and asks, "What are your kids doing? Cleaning?" If you have ever been to our house, you would know that it is always clean. If it's not clean, then that means my mom is not home. I do not know what we would do if she wasn't around. I'll be the first one to admit that without her, this family would likely fall apart fast!

I am such a daddy's girl, and I will always be. My dad and I love to spend time together, even if that means just going to the grocery store to pick up something for dinner. I will always drop what I am doing to join him because he is fun to be around and his jokes are kind of funny (even though half the time I say they aren't).

Daddy's little girl

Since he was a little kid, he loved surfing. He would head to the beach and surf for hours. That was back in the sixties when he says there were no crowds like today. He never surfed in any competitions; he did it for fun up until he was around sixty-four or sixty-five. Now his back hurts a bit and he doesn't surf anymore, but he watches a lot of surfing on the net. We all wish he would try getting back on his board again, but he says those days are over. He's played music since he was a child and now plays percussion in a band (or two), which he says charges his batteries these days.

As long as I can remember, dad has told me how much he loves the fact that I am his only girl. He always says, "You're my favorite daughter," and I always reply saying, "Well, yes, I am because I'm your only daughter." Being his only girl, he is very protective, and he worries about me a lot. Even though I am an adult now, he is still that same protective dad I knew when I was young. He wants to help me do a lot of things, but in reality, I am totally capable of doing most of those things myself.

During the Vietnam War (1965–1969) Dad was in the air force, working on cargo airplanes. Through social media like Facebook, he's been able to find guys who he served with, and he loves talking to them and reminiscing about surfing in Santa Cruz and driving home on weekends to play music. In 2000, he was diagnosed with breast cancer, and it was a tough experience for the entire family. Even though I was only seven years old, I remember seeing my dad in his room one afternoon while Mom was giving him a shot. I still remember the scream that my dad let out when he got that shot. It scared my mom so much that she quickly pulled the needle out and then had to put it back in again. He stayed strong the whole time, and he never gave up the fight. Now I can proudly say that my daddy is a cancer survivor. Since I was very young, my dad has always trusted me to do the right thing and encouraged me to be a good role model for my younger brother, Dewey. I don't know what I would do without my dad. I love both my parents very much.

Brad, my oldest brother, is my half-brother. We share the same dad, but have different moms. You probably would not have known this, because I don't differentiate when people ask how many brothers I have. I simply say three. I don't think of him as a half-brother. I just say he's my brother, plain and simple. Brad's mom is one of the nicest ladies. She's super funny, and I love getting to see her at family parties. My family has jokingly told me that I'm really her daughter because if you put us together, there really isn't much of a height difference. I don't have to look up as much to see her face. Even though my family gets a kick out of calling me her daughter, they are just kidding. I love Brad for the devoted and loving father that he has become since the birth of his daughter, Kirra. When we were growing up, I used to text him so I could bug him with my spelling. I would do it on purpose just so that he would correct me. We would end up laughing about it. Growing up, I don't see him much, but during the week, if I have a bad day at school, I will call or text him because I know that he can make me feel better. He makes everything seem like it will all be okay, and he is right. Right now I couldn't be more grateful and blessed for the people I am surrounded by. Brad's nickname for me is "Shorty." People might think I wouldn't like to be called that, but I don't mind. Brad is a very sweet, and caring person.

I am so glad that Brad and Molly met because they were meant for each other. I love Molly to death. She's the greatest sister-in-law anyone could ever ask for. She is very pretty, kind, and fits in perfectly with our family. When I first met her, she treated me like she would anybody else, and I loved that. I don't think she will ever know how much I love having her as a sister. I also love my niece and nephew so much. Even though I do not live close enough to see them very often, I do promise them that I will always be the best auntie and be there for them anytime they need me. I just pray that Kirra and Gavin have a happy and healthy life, will look up to me, and know that no matter what, I'll always love, protect, and care for them.

With Brad & Molly with niece and nephew Kirra and Gavin.

Since my brother Mitchell was four years old, he has been the wild child. He makes everyone laugh by saying or doing the weirdest things. When he was a little boy, he always went strolling around on his tricycle, dressed up with his cowboy boots and a funny outfit, yelling, "I'm going to ..." (He'd tell us wherever he wanted to go that very moment, which most of the time was Africa).

Mitch and I share a lot of memories, like the time when I was two and I couldn't walk or crawl. I would roll everywhere. I would chase him all around the house on the carpet and the tile floor. I tried to get him, and I never gave up. We would call this *steamroller,* and I was a pro at it! I could roll around corners and under people's feet. I rolled until I was three. I know I should have been walking by then, but I wasn't. Mitch would tease me, saying that I could never get him, but I know I did. He's now six foot two and a man who loves to live a reckless life. He's the kind of brother who always looks out for his siblings. He always says if I ever have a boyfriend, he doesn't want to see the guy anywhere close to the house. I feel safe when I am around him and so do a lot of other people. Whenever he is home for a visit, we have no worries leaving the front door open because nobody would mess with us if they saw him. I love him for being the great brother he was to me when I was younger, and I also love him for trying so hard to do the right thing in life. Everyone makes mistakes, and he made plenty of them, but it's not for me to judge. Mitch could tell you his life story, and you wouldn't believe it, because it's just crazy. Mitch just became a daddy to a beautiful baby boy, Vincent Mitchell Clark. The moment he found out that he was going to become a father, he was overjoyed and so happy. He loves his son so much. Little Vincent looks so much like his mommy and daddy. I'll always love Mitch.

Dewey! Dewey! Dewey! He is like any other nineteen-year-old boy who loves to annoy his older sister anytime he feels like it. When he's not home, the house becomes so quiet that it doesn't feel quite right. He loves to play all kinds of sports, but he mainly loves to surf. He goes to the beach with family or friends any chance he gets, and surfs until he gets tired or hungry. Dewey and I are very close. Of

27

course we fight and have our arguments, but we always love and care for one another. He plays the saxophone, and someday he may be a well-known jazz musician. He is just that good. I am always there to support him at every gig he has. I am the one swaying when it's jazz, tapping when he's playing other styles of music, or dancing when he's playing reggae, but I am always there. We have gone through a lot together during the last couple of years. We have always stuck by each other, and it has brought us closer together. It's really cute when he sticks up for me when someone is rude or mean to me. Even though he acts tough and crazy most of the time (especially if he has a friend around), he also has a sensitive side, and it's cute. Dewey gets that from my dad, who is the same way. Even though he had already bypassed me in height by the first grade, I felt I still needed to be that good older sister who he would look up to when he needed someone to talk with.

My family means the world to me, and they push me to do things that I thought I would never be able to do. Even though my family is far from being perfect, we love and care and just want the best for one another. Through all the hardships, I know my family will always stick together.

My protectors aka my brothers ♥

CHAPTER 5

The Trials of Elementary School Years

While all my classmates in third grade were growing and getting taller, I stayed the same height. I couldn't help but cry. I didn't want to be different. I didn't want to stay small. I wanted to grow and be like all the other boys and girls. *Unfair* was a word I understood very well. I always thought it was unfair that I was picked to be different. Why me? Why was I the one in this body that my classmates made fun of? Before I started attending school and the other kids started to grow, I was happy with myself. I didn't have to worry about what other people thought of me. When God had all the other boys and girls start to grow taller and I stayed the same, I couldn't hide anymore. I was standing alone in this classroom, having to deal with everybody's confusion. I was confused too. I was wondering, *Is this really true?* I knew it wasn't a dream so of course it was true, but it never seemed fair.

From pre-kindergarten to the end of third grade, I attended Burroughs Elementary and made friends with a lot of the kids in my classes. Some were really nice and never saw me as different. Others couldn't come to grips with the fact that I was the same as anybody else. Some kids opened their mouths a little too often and asked some hurtful and rude questions.

The first time I remember somebody making fun of me at school was in third grade. It was recess time, and everyone was playing different games. Like anyone else, I was really good at some games and not so good at other ones. I was always good at handball, tetherball, volleyball, and hide-and-seek. I loved to play and run around with all my friends. The playground was large enough so that when we played tag, no one could ever catch the other person. Playground time was fun because when I wanted to walk around with a friend, we could walk in one direction until we got tired and then turn around and walk back to where we started.

Everyone loved to sit on or hang from the monkey bars. Since I couldn't reach them, I would stand there and watch everyone else play. I wasn't allowed to hang from them because I could get hurt and it was bad for my joints. One time a few friends picked me up and let me grab the bar so that I could feel the same kind of thrill that everyone else was feeling. On another occasion, I was pretending to have a good time, watching everyone else play, when a third grade boy sitting on the monkey bars asked me, "Why can't you go on the monkey bars?" I told him that it was bad for my joints, and he started laughing and making fun of me. I took it hard and started crying. Some of my friends who witnessed the whole thing stuck up for me and told the boy he was mean. As I was walking to my classroom with my friends, I saw my teacher, and she asked why I was crying. I told her what had happened, and the principal got involved.

In third grade, I joined the YMCA swim team to meet new people and to have something to do in my free time. On Tuesdays and Thursdays, I would carpool to the YMCA to swim laps with my lifelong friend and "sister," Veronica LeBrun. I began to really enjoy swimming and competing against other kids. It was great exercise and challenged me in a number of different ways. When I first signed up to be a part of the swim team, I was nervous that I would be the slowest swimmer because my arms and legs were half as long as everyone else's. Even though I wanted to be treated equally, I knew the coaches might not have a clue about what I could do or how long I could do it. After my mom talked to the couple in charge, I wasn't so nervous anymore. They agreed to have me use fins when practicing and competing so it would be an equal competition. Putting those fins on made me feel like I was swimming fifty miles per hour. I felt like a brand-new person. Gliding through the water made me feel free; it made me feel like no one could ever tell me that I couldn't do something. I am extremely grateful that the YMCA understood my needs and made adaptations, and that I got the chance to be on a swim team and learn what it's like to compete against other kids my age. Some parents thought it was unfair that their baby was racing against someone with fins on. To those parents, I encourage your baby to walk a mile in my shoes.

Third grade came to an end when my parents told me they were going to move me to a small private school for fourth grade. It was sad to know that I wouldn't be able to be at the same school with my close friends. It was not easy to say good-bye to everyone, especially one of my best friends, Cynthia. We had become inseparable. She was the sister that I never had, and was the one who would defend me when I was bullied. I would often wish to go back to those days when we use to hang out every day after school. I miss her, and those memories that we shared are really special to me. She is the main reason why I missed attending that school, but I certainly didn't miss all the bullying that went on there. After I left and moved on, it made it hard for Cynthia and I to get together and have our play dates.

Some of my other friends that I would hang out with at recess and after school were Bailey, Richard, Roger, Jade, and Tyler. I wish I could see them again because I miss all of them so much, and they were a huge part of my life in elementary school.

When fourth grade came around, I met new friends, but of course I had to answer more questions about my short stature. My parents thought it would be best for me to attend the new school because my younger brother, Dewey, was already there. Even though it was cool to go to the same school as him, I wasn't thrilled knowing

I had to start making new friends and answering questions. This was also the year I stopped growing. From that point in my life, I had to become a stronger person, both spiritually and mentally. I had to learn that people aren't always going to be friendly.

It was in fourth grade I felt for the first time that there were going to be some days when I'd want to give up. I knew I couldn't, though, and learned that I had to keep my head up high and keep going. I didn't know then who to look to in times of sadness and sorrow, besides my family, so that year I asked God to come into my life. From then on, I have been walking with Him and have been dedicating my life to Him. I can't remember what it was like not having Him in my life because it feels so long ago. I've been much happier since I let God take control of my life, and I've relaxed in the passenger seat.

I grew up camping at different beaches with these
three; Luke, Dewey, me and Hannah.

I don't pretend to have all the answers to life's big questions, such as why God chose me to be the person in this smaller body, but I do know God has a perfect reason behind why He did that. Until I find out what His plan is for my life, I'll just wait to see.

Though God has a plan and purpose for everyone's life, there are some instances where you may wonder why He had certain things happen. These instances may stick with you until the day you die. I will never forget one. It pops into my mind at the most random times. In the summer of 2005, I was twelve and I had two weeks to relax on the sand and swim in the ocean of Hawaii. I spent quality time with my family, and drove all around the island of Kauai looking for great surf spots. Joining in on the fun for a week were my family's closest friends, Cindy and Ralph, whom I love very much. My brothers and I call them our aunt and uncle because they played a big role in our lives growing up. Cindy and my mom met in middle school, and they've been best friends ever since.

The love I have for these two is indescribable.
My Aunt Cindy and Uncle Ralph.

One of those days really stands out to me. It was sunny, and my dad, Dewey, and Mitch were out surfing. My uncle took a break from surfing so he could swim around with me on an inner tube in the warm water. My mom and aunt were on the sand, laughing and having a great time. When my uncle and I were out a little ways, I saw a man swimming laps a little farther out, but I didn't think much about the guy. The next thing I knew, the same man was swimming right toward us. I didn't know who he was. I thought he would just swim right past us, but instead he stopped when he got close enough to talk to Uncle Ralph. He told my uncle that he shouldn't let me swim in the ocean because I might drown. I could tell that Ralph wasn't happy. He didn't understand why this man, out of the blue, just swam up to us and started talking like he was a lifeguard. My uncle then told him, "I have it all under control. She knows how to swim fine, and she won't drown." The man continued to argue with Uncle Ralph about the situation while I was floating and watching all of this, but a couple minutes later, he went back to swimming his laps.

Kauai Vacation 2005

35

If someone thinks I can't do something because of my height, I'll always try and do my best. If it doesn't work out, then I know it's not what I'm meant to do. I knew back then I could swim and tread water, so there wasn't anything to worry about, plus my uncle was right there next to me if anything happened. But thanks, anyway, to the guy for his concern.

Stand Up Paddle in Hawaii

Not all my childhood memories are sad or are of me getting teased and laughed at. I have a lot of great memories of being an older sister to Dewey, and a younger sister to both Mitch and Brad. I don't like to think about all the bad memories that I may have had in the past. Instead, I love to focus on all of the good and uplifting ones, and on my future.

I may be half Dewey's size, but I am still his older sister. I was two when my parents brought Dewey home from the hospital. I loved being a big sister because I got to boss him around and pretend to be his mother, and he hated every second of it. Even though I made him mad, I always stuck up for him when he got in trouble and would cry if he were put into his room for time out. As Dewey's older sister, I did what he asked me to do. Even though I had a lot of different experiences out in the world while growing up, I had a happy childhood at home.

CHAPTER 6

The Importance of LPA

L PA is Little People of America. It's life changing. Fun. Amazing. Indescribable. LPA is an organization that has had an impact on me in a way that is hard to explain. It is an organization that I have been a part of my whole life.

Friends; Brittany, Elizabeth, me and Jonny

On its official website, LPA describes itself as a nonprofit organization that provides support and information to people of short stature and their families all over the world. There are over six thousand members in the United States and internationally. LPA is divided into thirteen regional districts, and seventy local chapters. I live in District 12, which covers California, Hawaii, and Nevada. The local chapters in District 12 include Los Angeles, Orange County, San Diego, Sacramento, San Joaquin Valley, and the San Francisco Bay Area.

Each district and local chapter organizes activities throughout the year. Orange County has outings; family gatherings; seasonal events at Easter, Halloween, Christmas; and a summer beach party. Twice a year, one of the chapters in my district has a weekend event called a *regional*, where people drive or fly into a city, usually somewhere in California, and stay in a huge hotel. For my age group, the regionals are mainly for hanging out with new or old friends whom you might not have seen since the last regional. You hang by the pool and have fun. At night, there is a dance that everyone looks forward to, and everyone in attendance gets all dressed up. They are always so much fun.

In the summer, rotating in a different state each year, one of the LPA chapters hosts a week of activities known as a *national*. People from all around the world come together for a week of fun, meeting new people, staying up until the early hours of the morning, and competing in the DAAA National Games.

DAAA stands for Dwarf Athletic Association of America, and it provides an opportunity for dwarfs to compete in a bunch of sports, such as track and field athletics, basketball, football, bocce, swimming, table tennis, badminton, volleyball, and soccer. It's nice to be able to compete in a sport that you love and want to play in school, but can't because it's too dangerous competing against average-stature people. With the DAAA, there aren't any worries of it being too dangerous because everyone is around the same size and height. Even though I love all of the sports, I don't compete in everything. The main DAAA sports I participate in are swimming, track and field, and bocce. When I am not playing, I'll always show up to the different events and cheer on my friends. I love to go and just watch everyone else play.

During the week of the national, when we are off doing our thing, there are different workshops for young teens, parents, siblings, or even friends of a little person to attend to learn more about dwarfism and better understand what we go through on a daily basis. The whole week is so much fun because of how organized and jam-packed with activities it is. Not only are there DAAA sports to participate in, but there is also a talent/fashion show, movie night, teen meetings, kids camp, and dances each night, ending in the early hours of the morning. The week is very special for most of us because it is a time when we can get to know someone who we might want to get married to in the future. It is a time to meet people and connect with them, so when we leave, we can still keep in touch by phone, text, e-mail, Facebook, and Skype. It can be really hard to live across the state or country from a person whom you may grow to call boyfriend, girlfriend, or simply friend. It can be months before you get the opportunity to see them again in person.

Living it up at the LPA National with these girls!

One of my absolute favorite things that I have gained from this organization is an endless amount of friends. These people know me inside and out and often have been through issues similar to ones that

I may be dealing with. These are the people I go to for advice on how to approach new situations and experiences. These are the people who keep me focused on what life is really about. There are many women I look up to and admire in LPA. From every conversation we share about guys, marriages, and babies, I always feel hopeful about what is to come in the future. I have little people friends from all over the United States as well as from different countries, such as Switzerland, Australia, and even Egypt. It can be amazing to visit them because you get to experience how they live, and you always know there will be a step stool there just waiting for you. Since travel can be expensive, however, the best chance to reconnect with your friends face-to-face is at these little people conventions. In LPA, you gain life-long friends who you'll love and cherish forever. We definitely know the true value of our time together and always make the absolute best of it. LPA is so amazing, and I think it's one of the greatest organizations I'll ever be a part of.

In Seattle for the LPA convention

October has officially become Dwarfism Awareness Month, and it gets me super excited every time I think about it. I love how every month has a different cause to help us to become more aware. Aside from October being Dwarfism Awareness Month, it is also National Breast Cancer and Liver Cancer Awareness Month, Down Syndrome and Domestic Violence Awareness Month, National Physical Therapy Month (this one is for you Mark and Amber), and so many others. I hope you can help me and every other individual educate the world. I get excited every time October rolls around, and I hope you start to as well.

CHAPTER 7

Another New Start:
Middle School

I stepped away from a school with children who finally got to know what it's like to be in a class with a dwarf. These friends didn't look at me like I was an alien. Now I had to move on to a new school with students who had never seen a person with dwarfism before and who did not know what to expect when they saw me. With a new school comes new faces, many questions, friendships, and a bunch of kids wondering why I am so short. Despite these challenges, all I could say the night before I started middle school was, "I'm ready!"

For some people, going to a new school is a very hard thing to do. Some of you who are reading this now are possibly experiencing this sense of anxiety at the moment. If you're worried about middle or high school, there are four things that I have learned and encourage you to keep in mind:

1. It doesn't matter if you have one great friend or ten. What does matter is how they make you feel, and whether or not they are a great influence in your life. Do you feel inspired

by them? Do they make you feel good about yourself or do they tear you down and make you feel worthless?

2. Know what's ahead. You should have things planned that you're looking forward to. Set goals and dreams for your life, and reach out for them. If you don't have anything to look forward to then some days it might seem as if you don't have anything to live for.

3. Always know that the amount of effort you put into school or work will certainly pay off. I was a slow learner in middle school and still am to this day, so studying for tests never comes easy for me. I could study for hours and hours only to earn a B or C for my efforts. I worked hard in school, though, and made sure I showed all my teachers how hard I was trying. Someone once asked me if I deserved the grades I received, and I said certainly not. I didn't deserve them because I had studied so hard and never missed a single homework assignment. I believe that I should have been rewarded for my efforts. Now that I am older, I see all of the hard work I put into my studies throughout the years is finally paying off.

4. Lastly, if you're having a bad day at school or if someone is being mean to you, remember that you have people who love and care about you. Some call those people family, and others call those people their mentors or friends. For those of you who are feeling lost and alone, never, ever give up. Never lose hope, and know things will get better no matter what you are going through at the moment.

When I was in sixth grade, and almost ready to graduate from my elementary school, Brethren Christian, I tried out for cheerleading for the upcoming school year at the middle school. After the long try out, I waited for a few days until the coaches decided who would be on the team. I finally got an e-mail from the cheer coach listing all the names of those that made the squad. I scoured the list, one name at a time, before coming to the last name and realizing that Madi

Clark was not on the list. It was okay and I was still so happy for all of the other girls who had made the squad because I knew that I would return the next year and give cheerleading a second try.

As I packed my bag with pencils, pens, cute little highlighters, and everything else that I might need for my first day of middle school, my mom reminded me that she had already given my new teachers the letter. When she said that, I knew exactly what she was talking about. My mom had me read the letter so I could have a say in whether or not I liked it. Previously, a mother of another little person had composed a letter to give to every teacher her daughter would have in school. She was generous enough to send it to any parent of a little person who requested it. Of course, my mom wanted a copy, so when it was time for me to enter each grade from kindergarten to ninth, my teachers and my school's administration got a better understanding of what dwarfism was. The first page of the letter is simply about me and how I'm capable of doing anything that the other kids do, and that I need little help because I need to learn how to be independent. It stated that I need to learn to find ways of accomplishing certain tasks that I'm going to face in life.

It continues, "Please let Madi do as many things on her own as possible. We want her to be independent. Sometimes this may mean finding a creative way for her to reach something or to do a task. It is usually as simple as her using a stool to stand on." It was sort of a harsh reality in a way. I knew I wanted to be treated the same, but then again, the thought of maybe getting away with something, such as skipping a homework assignment just because they felt sorry for me, was kind of intriguing. Since that letter didn't say that my teachers should feel sorry for me or give me a break if I didn't do my homework, they did not feel the need to do that. They treated me like any other student in the class. They called on me to read or answer a question even when I didn't want to and had me do all the homework and projects that everyone else was assigned. If I didn't do those things, then my grade was going to be marked down. My parents were concerned about sending me off to teachers who had no clue about dwarfism, so the letter's second page was full of the facts to know about dwarfism, such as, "Any amount of force on her wrist (holding hands) or any effort to pull her arms could easily cause her joints to become dislocated."

A week before my big day, my mom took me so I could see where all my classes were located. When I began on the first day of school, I didn't get lost or confused. Being in middle school meant having my very own locker to decorate and a class schedule that rotated between different rooms, so I wouldn't be stuck in one classroom the whole day. When I arrived at the school with my mom, I didn't know what to expect or whom we were going to meet. The teachers were in their classes getting ready for a new school year, and the cheerleaders were outside practicing for a new cheer season. As I walked through the front doors of Valley Christian and turned right, I noticed that there were two rows of lockers: one row on top and one on the bottom. As I was searching for my locker, I hoped that the school would know that I was coming and give me a bottom one. There was absolutely no way that I would be able to reach the top locker, not even if I jumped or got on my tiptoes. I walked down the hall in search of my locker number, and unfortunately, it was one of those on top. Wondering what I should do next, I called my friend, Kelsey. She told me that she received a bottom one and asked if I wanted to switch with her. Of course I said yes. So she gave me my new locker combination, and I was ready to decorate and hang pictures and inspirational quotes and install a hot pink shelf and other cute little accessories in there. I was not focusing on anything else. I was simply in my own little world. At the end of the day, Kelsey and I were both happy. I got my bottom locker, and she got her top. We didn't have to bend down or reach up for any of our books.

A lady walked up to my mom and me and introduced herself. I would have never guessed how much of a blessing and an impact she would have on my life for that year and the years to come. Her name was Bonnie De Jong. When Mrs. De Jong learned that a student with dwarfism would be joining VCMS, she had her husband research more about the topic. Her efforts made me grateful that there are people out there who are curious enough to learn more about dwarfism.

The first day of school felt like a total blur. All I was focused on when I first got up that morning was getting through the day and surviving my first day of middle school. My memory isn't so clear when it comes to all the studying and the tests I had, but I do have a great memory about all the happy and sad times in my life. So not really being able to remember my first day of middle school makes me believe that I was in my own little world that day. Friends of mine come up to me and tell me that I was one of the first people to smile and say hello to them. I feel bad because I really don't remember meeting them or anyone that entire blurry day.

A couple of days into the new school year, I started really loving things at Valley. I never wanted to leave. I felt like the weekends were going by so slowly and I couldn't wait to get to school on Monday—it couldn't come fast enough. It's strange to think that a teenager could love school that much, but I did. Sending me there was one of the best decisions my parents ever made for me.

In seventh grade, with the help of Mrs. De Jong, I started to learn what kind of a person I wanted to become. She helped me find that person buried deep inside of me. If it weren't for her, I wouldn't have been thinking of what I wanted for my life at such a young age. Since my school is a private school, we had chapel once a week. During that time, the whole school gathered together and worshiped the Lord, learned about Him, and listened to a guest speaker talk and tell a story. While in seventh grade, Mrs. De Jong set up a chapel session for me so that I could talk about dwarfism. She made a movie called *Hey, Madi!,* and I was blessed to be a part of that. I enjoyed getting in front of my middle school classmates and teachers to talk about the subject that I'm most comfortable with. From then on, I knew I was meant to share my story with kids and adults around the world. I surely hope that I get more opportunities to do so in the future.

At the end of seventh grade, I gave cheerleading another try, and I made it! Overall, my first year of middle school was fun and went by very quickly. In eighth grade, new teachers were assigned to me, and

Mom sent out letters again. Just like the previous year, my teachers didn't cut me any slack. My parents enrolled Dewey at my middle school, and I looked forward to him again being in the same school. It was cool seeing him at breaks and at lunch, but I knew whenever he came to talk to me, it was usually to ask me if he could borrow some money. When he asks for anything, it's hard to tell him no, so I always gave in.

CHAPTER 8

Entering High School: New Challenges

As I got out of my mom's car the morning of my first day of high school, I was nervous. I was nervous about what the upperclassmen would think of me, and nervous about possibly walking into the wrong classroom. I was fearful that I might be late to my classes because of the fact that it takes me longer to get from one place to another. For the most part, though, I was excited to see what high school had to offer. I would now be on the school campus, walking the same halls every Monday through Friday for the next four years. Luckily, the campus wasn't too big. It was a perfect size for me, and it was easy enough for me to get around and get from class to class on time.

The night before school started, a wave of anxiety came over me. I broke into tears and told my parents that there was no way I was going to school the next morning. There was no possible way they could make me go. I had received a phone call the night before from a friend who warned me that it was going to be "the worst day of our lives." She conjured up the image that all the upperclassmen would be mean and give us a hard time. Looking back, we both feel foolish for crying and worrying so much about the older kids and what we thought they would do to us as new students. My parents calmed me down and convinced me that everything would be fine. I went to school with all my letters to give to my teachers, just as I did in middle school. I gave the letters to them, either at the beginning of the class before the bell rang or right after, when everyone was leaving. I didn't want anyone to see me giving them letters because I just didn't want to answer any questions regarding what they were about.

It turns out that my first day was not bad at all; in fact, it turned out to be really good. The friend who told me it was going to be a challenging day had no clue what it would be like. All the upperclassmen were truly so nice. It seems like each minute that passed, a new person came up to me to introduce themselves. I didn't know why I was the one everyone wanted to meet, though it was likely a bit of curiosity. Don't get me wrong, I absolutely love meeting new people and being friends with everyone, but I didn't want any special treatment. I wanted to simply blend in with my surroundings, but it's difficult to do that when you are unequivocally the shortest person on campus.

The school day was made up of seven different periods, which meant there were seven different classes we would have to go to. Wednesday and Thursday were the exception, when there were only three or four. Each first period in the first semester, I would say hi to the sweetest upperclassman. Her name was Emily, and she was a junior. I was in English class, and she was right across the hall in Spanish class. Both teachers would keep the door open for a little while, and we both sat by the door of the classrooms, so saying good morning or smiling to each other in the beginning of class was something we did every day. It made every morning that first semester very special for me.

Once a year at Valley, a student's counselor meets with them for a quick five-minute meeting. The meeting is called a "grad check." The main purpose of a grad check is to look over the student's grades and talk about where the student is hoping to go to college. During freshman year, a grad check is a way to tell your counselor what your goals are for the next four years and perhaps what you want your major to be in college. During my grad check, my counselor told me how excited she was that I was attending Valley Christian High. She said if I needed anything at all that I should come back and talk to her.

As the days went by, I found that the toilets in the bathrooms were at an okay height for me, but the paper towel dispensers were a bit too high. Every girl in the school must have a friend accompany her to the bathroom. That is a school rule for everyone. So, reaching the paper towels was no big deal because I could always ask my friend to get some down for me. I have no problem asking people for help, unless I feel like the person is getting irritated with me for asking repeatedly. Anyone I asked was kind enough to help me whenever I needed. I went back into the counselor's office later that year, and she told me she had heard I couldn't reach the paper towels. I confirmed, and she asked which bathroom I used the most. She arranged to have accommodations made by installing a lower paper towel dispenser. The custodial staff went above and beyond as the lower dispenser was installed in every bathroom on campus. I was overjoyed and so grateful that the school would do that for me. Now if another little person comes to my school in the future, high paper towel dispensers will not be a problem for them. I can't thank Valley Christian enough for making my life a little easier.

The school year continued, and I became friends with a lot of incredible people. Some I'm still friends with, and some I am not connected to anymore. To this day, I miss those friends, many whom I seemed to talk to 24/7. I wish we could be close again, but there must be a reason they aren't in my life any longer. It is sad to lose friends, but that's life. Friends come and go, but my family is always a constant for me. Freshman year went by very fast, and it was hard to think that the next three years would go by just as quickly.

Sophomore year arrived, and it was a whole lot easier than my freshman year because I already knew everyone. The first day of school, my teachers informed me that they had a surprise for me. When I walked into their classroom, each one pulled out and pointed to a stool. When sitting at a desk using an average chair, my legs go numb or fall asleep because I can't rest them on the floor. By using a stool along with an averaged-sized chair, my legs no longer dangle. I felt a sense of relief knowing that the rest of my high school experience would be a little less painful. Being in physical pain distracts me from learning, and sometimes when I try to stand up, I can't walk because my legs are numb. Having stools in each classroom was a big help, and I was happy about that.

Being asked to a high school dance would seem like no big deal for most girls, but being the girl that never got asked was heart wrenching. Sophomore year, I asked my friend, who was also a little person, to join me, and we had a lot of fun. I was asked later in the year by another friend, Jonny, to his prom, and of course I said yes. He's like a brother to me, and I absolutely love his family. As great as the evening was, trying to find a prom dress was a bit difficult. Normal dresses are easy to find since many of them are short to begin with and go to my knees. Prom dresses are usually long, so they need to be altered and hemmed. When I found the dress I liked, it took a week to hem it, but we took it in two weeks before the prom to be sure it would be finished in time. When the alterations were complete, I tried my dress on and I couldn't have been happier. It fit great and was fabulous for my first prom.

There weren't any problems with kids teasing me about my height at Valley. It became like a second home to me. But because I don't get teased at home and I didn't get teased at school, I did worry when I was away from one of my homes that there was a possibility teasing could occur.

People may have made fun of me at school behind my back, but not once did they taunt me to my face. It can be a cruel world. People often tease others for looking different, being overweight, being gay or lesbian, or having some sort of eating disorder. This is disappointing. We never know what the other person is going through each day and should think before saying anything rude or offensive. As the saying goes, walk a mile in another man's shoes before passing judgment.

When my junior year started, I had an open mind and knew that anything could happen. I stepped back onto the campus of Valley Christian High, ready to see what the year would throw at me, and I was ready to walk through whatever door opened for me. As it turned out, though, nothing could have prepared me for what I experienced in eleventh grade. It was by far the toughest year, and it was one of the most depressing years.

The homework wasn't the only thing that made my year hard. It was the process of finding myself, accepting who I am as an individual, and knowing that I can't change who I am on the outside. Though I thought I had already worked through that in middle school when Mrs. De Jong helped me out, things happened that challenged me in a different way and made me sit back and wonder whether or not I was okay in this smaller body. I felt a lot of sadness that year and was very depressed, to the point that I was crying myself to sleep most nights. I tried to figure things out on my own, but I really needed someone by my side to help me. Some days I was happy and other days sad, angry, and just not myself. I hated feeling angry, not just toward myself, but also toward my family and friends. I wanted to be happy, but it was extremely hard to feel that way. I hid a lot of what I was feeling behind my smile. I smiled a lot so that whoever I came in contact with would think everything was okay; but I was living a big lie. Some days I was even lying to myself, trying to believe that what I was feeling was really nothing and that it would go away if I smiled just a little bit more. The discussion of home school was brought up a lot in my house. I wanted to leave my high school because I was no longer happy there. The truth was I was just not happy with myself.

My parents had a meeting with my counselor and a few other teachers to discuss leaving Valley Christian, and being homeschooled came up. I don't think my teachers could believe that this was how I was feeling because it seemed like everything was okay. I had a meeting with my school counselor. She told me that it was okay to be sad, but I needed to be able to talk about my feelings more. I excel at talking about my feelings. I learned it was good for me to open up and express myself and not hold everything inside. Holding things in was becoming way too much to handle. Part of my problem was that I sought a whole lot of love and attention from my family, but I felt they weren't giving me all the love and attention that I needed.

I have come to understand that this is my life, and I shouldn't let what people say about me get me down. The truth is, everyone is different and handles their own pain and sorrow in their own way. Yes, I'm a little person, and yes, I love being one, but some days I can't believe this is really my life.

CHAPTER 9

Class of 2012

Senior year! I feel like I was a freshman such a short time ago, looking up to all the older kids, and now I'm the old kid that all the freshman theoretically look up to. It's amazing for me to believe that I'm a senior because I never thought I would make it this far without giving up. I never saw myself as a senior, especially after going through such a challenging junior year. It certainly helped to stay busy and keep my mind off things that might bother me.

I joined school choir, and that was definitely a neat experience since I never had the guts to try out before. One of the reasons I decided to try out was because I knew people in the Broadway Showcase last year and became inspired to be involved in a musical experience. Broadway Showcase highlights the musical talent and commitment of Valley Christian School's students in grades one to twelve. Each year it is held at the La Mirada Theatre for the Performing Arts. In preparation for the show, everyone in charge teaches, inspires, and encourages the students involved to attain more than they thought they could possibly do by themselves. The show displays scenes from Broadway musicals and allows each choir to demonstrate their ability and unique skills. Each student sings, dances, and exudes an enormous amount of stage presence. I heard so many wonderful things about Broadway Showcase and how everyone has so much fun learning the dances and singing the songs that I knew I wanted to give it a try.

The senior formal and prom was incredibly fun because I went with a great group of people. I have made a name for myself around campus for tripping and falling. I fall at least once a week (no joke), and this year at school I have had some bad falls. Each time I had to walk away laughing or else I'd likely cry. While walking back to the party bus at formal, I realized that I hadn't fallen yet, but I guess I spoke too soon. Just as I was thinking that, I tripped over a curb and fell on the sidewalk. I am not completely sure why that curb was there because it seriously looked like it was placed right in the middle of the walkway so that I would fall over it. As I fell, my purse went soaring, and my dress went flying up. My friend, Kalei, who played the role of superhero of the night, reached down before anyone could see my butt and fixed my dress for me. Unfortunately, she went flying on top of me, and there we were, two girls lying in the middle of the sidewalk in prom gowns, laughing so hard we nearly cried. People started picking up our stuff and helped us up, but we both walked away from there with bruises and scrapes on our arms and legs. It was definitely a night that we will never forget, and I will somehow continue to laugh about it.

Every Wednesday morning, all of the students go into the gym to worship and hear a guest speaker talk about a specific topic. On Wednesday, February 15th, the entire school made their way into the gym to hear *me* speak, and tell *my* story. I had the privilege of standing in front of my whole school and telling them what it's like to be a little person. We started that morning with three worship songs, and while I was singing, my heart wouldn't stop pounding. I knew that I would soon walk on stage, and I was praying that God would calm my nerves. I've spoken to a crowd of people before, sharing with them the obstacles that I face on a daily basis and how I overcome them. The only difference this time was that I was speaking to my friends. Most of these friends, classmates, and school faculty had not heard my story before; they didn't know what it was like to walk in my shoes. They soon found out. I knew before I got up there that I wanted to share personal things and not hold anything back. I wanted everyone to hear what was in my heart, and I'm happy to say that they did.

There were portions where I spoke seriously, and then there were parts where I slid in a couple jokes. There were a couple of times while I was being asked questions by a teacher who sat on stage with me that I felt tears running down my chin. I closed with some final words on what I hoped they'd take from my story, and then I was done. At that moment, my entire school gave me a standing ovation. It started when one boy stood up clapping, and then everyone else started standing and clapping. Words can't describe what it felt like watching everyone stand up. I wasn't expecting anything like that to happen. It brought tears to my eyes, and I won't ever forget that moment because it meant so much to me. From the feedback that I received, everyone seemed to love the chapel, and they all got something out of it. I had the privilege of meeting so many new faces around my campus as a result of my speech. It's great to know that the people who used to refrain from speaking to me are now comfortable coming up to me to say, "Hey." Everyone has a unique story of their own to tell, and hopefully I'll have many more opportunities to speak to individuals about what it feels like being judged.

During my senior year, I decided to sign up for my first mission trip to Zuni, New Mexico. I did not know what to expect, but I learned that going into things like this, you shouldn't expect anything. I try to go into everything with an open heart and open mind. There were twenty-five of us who gathered that early Saturday morning to pack our stuff in cars and take off for a six-day trip to Zuni. Most of the group had gone before, but there were a couple of us who were experiencing this for the very first time. It is hard to put into words everything that I experienced. The kids who lived in Zuni were wonderful, and seeing them smiling brought so much joy. It was also amazing to get away from the Internet, all the media, and everything that distracts us on a daily basis. At school, we get caught up with the things around us and never actually stop and relax. Each day in Zuni, we spent thirty minutes talking with God and working on a daily devotion. The trip was exactly what I needed. I'm sad that was my last year going, and I encourage everyone to go on some kind of mission trip sometime in their life. Not only will you be a blessing to the ones you're working with, but the ones you're working with will also bless you.

As senior year came to an end, I graduated and went off to college. I will most likely never again see most of the people I graduated with. Spending the last year with them made it special, and I can confidently say it was one of my best years yet. It was simply amazing in so many ways.

I regret that I hadn't gotten to know many of them better before we had to say good-bye in June. My senior year was really neat because I came out of my shell and showed a different side of myself. I often get quiet and have my guard up when I am around certain people, but other times I can be totally loud. Several people had tried to explain to me what senior year would be like, but I didn't really understand completely until I experienced it. They all said, "It goes by fast, so enjoy it," and they were right. I will likely share the same message with the underclassmen: "Enjoy your senior year because it goes by fast." It's totally true!

When I thought about graduating and how I would no longer see the kids that I'd been seeing every day at school, it made me reflect on my hopes and concerns about leaving VCHS. I hoped that when I left, I would find my way in this incredibly big world. It excited me to think I'd be more independent, and I wouldn't have to let family know where I was or what I was doing every second. It excited me to think I was going to be meeting so many more incredible people in college, and that it was just the beginning of a really good rest of my life. Knowing that I wouldn't have my mom and dad with me everywhere I'd go or have them sticking up for me made me feel a bit intimidated. It also made me nervous to think my parents would one day be saying, "You know what, it's time for you to pay your own phone bill, rent, car insurance, groceries, and everything else we've provided for you for some time now." I couldn't wait to see what door God opened for me next, and how my relationship with God would improve as the years went on.

As I look back, I've learned not to take anything for granted. I appreciate how you should cherish every minute that you spend here on earth. All you have is this moment, so stop waiting for better days. Quit saying, "I'll do it tomorrow." Who knows what tomorrow will bring? We don't even know what the next hour will bring. We should try to live each day as if it might be our last.

CHAPTER 10

Physical Aspects

*M*adi runs? Madi can do sports? Madi is not a runner because she can't run fast enough to keep up with everyone. Madi can't play sports because sports are for taller people. So what can Madi do? Well, I can be a part of any sports team that I want to be a part of, and can do anything that anyone else can do. I really wish it were just that simple. I can't quite be a part of any sports team that I want, considering my short stature and my bones. Even though my motto is, "I can do anything that anyone else can, but maybe just in a different way," sometimes, the truth of the matter is, I simply can't. My safety always comes first, no matter what. Had I decided to play sports, such as soccer, basketball, and cheerleading, then just maybe people around school would know me as the girl who proved everyone wrong instead of simply being recognized as the smallest girl on campus. If I were given a chance to change things, one thing I know I'd change would be to have been involved in those sports.

Took Adaptive Skiing lessons in Big Bear, CA

It's tough enough to play sports in high school, but what's even more difficult is trying to play basketball when you come up to everyone else's butts! The thought of being able to do something so tough is exhilarating and inspiring to me. The only thing that held me back from going out for basketball was my limitations. Limitations means putting a restriction on something, "a condition of limited ability." The only thing that limits me is the pain I endure on a daily basis as I try to participate in certain physical tasks. When my body says, "No more," I listen to it and stop.

So you may ask, "Are people with dwarfism able to participate in athletic activities?" The answer is, yes, within the limits of our individual medical diagnoses. For instance, swimming and bicycling are great for people with skeletal dysplasia since those activities put minimal pressure on the spine. Long-distance running and contact sports can be harmful due to the potential of significant pressure or impact on the spine.

I live to workout!

Not everyone realizes how tough it really is to walk both short and long distances while trying to keep up with the ones who we're walking with. Often, my legs will begin to hurt and I'll need to sit down for a minute and take a break. When I go to Target, I often have to take a little break on a low shelf or anywhere I can sit down just for a minute. When I'm at Disneyland with friends who want to walk all around the park, I get tired and feel pain, and all I want to do is sit down.

When I was in middle school, I had Bonnie De Jong as a Phys. Ed. coach. She was aware of what I could and could not do, and made sure that I was treated as fairly as all the other girls. Once a week, the entire class had to run a mile, which consisted of four laps around the track. Since my legs are half as long as everyone else's, and one step for them was two steps for me, Mrs. De Jong had me run half of it, or only two laps. My fellow classmates probably complained that I only had to do half but, really, it was fair because for me that's the equivalent of a full mile. In the middle of the year, I set a goal for myself that by the end of the year, I would run or walk all four laps. I just wanted to show everyone I could do it so they would all stop complaining. At the end of the year, I proclaimed to Mrs. De Jong, "I'm doing it!" And I did. I'll never forget that moment when I finished. It was amazing that when some of my classmates finished running their mile, they came and finished my mile with me. It's something I'll never forget.

I was kind of nervous when I had to take PE my freshman year of high school because I had no clue whether my teacher would be accepting of my needs. I wondered if she were to see me hurting whether she would just tell me to run some more. My teacher was Mrs. Streelman, and on the first day of school, I gave her the letter that my mom wrote to her and all my other teachers. That letter prompted her to research my condition and see what health benefits and health cautions she should provide in the next four years as my PE coach. I hated being treated differently, and I was afraid of what the others in my class would think. When Mrs. Streelman told the class to do something, she would then modify or give me an alternate workout to do. I didn't want to be seen as taking the easy way out, so I would outwardly complain, while in the back of my head I would say, *Thank you*. She pushed me like everyone else, but she took my aching joints into consideration. We have shared a lot of valuable conversations, and many of them left us both crying.

I'll never forget the time when I was working out, and she asked if I felt sore. When I replied, "Yes!" she said, "Yeah, everyone else is sore too." If that didn't make me stop feeling sorry for myself then I don't know what would have. I need to remember that even though my bones may hurt from walking, there are far greater struggles that other people are facing. I am truly blessed that both Bonnie De Jong and Erica Streelman came into my life because they've not only taught me so much about what physical things I can and cannot do, they've taught me so much about myself and about life in general.

CHAPTER 11

Spread Hope; Share a Smile

I am always nice to strangers, even though my parents taught me at a young age not to talk to them. I knew that was nearly impossible for me to do because I am so outgoing. I love to say hi, smile, or even start up a conversation with different people that I do not know because I enjoy meeting and getting to know people from all walks of life. Making someone else smile makes me want to smile too. You never know if the person is having a bad day or if they are feeling down. Who knows if they feel as if no one loves them and they have no reason to live a moment longer? A smile might keep them going; maybe it will show them that people do care. Maybe by smiling it will give them *hope*.

When I am feeling down, I look to other people to give me hope. Receiving a smile from someone can do wonders and can brighten up my day tremendously. Who have you smiled at today?

The absolute best place for me to meet new people is at the gym. I can't believe how many people I have met there and how many conversations I have had at the gym, with men and women of all ages. It is really fun to walk by someone, smile, and then see them stop what they are doing and look at me. They probably cannot believe a little person smiled at them. As I keep walking, I can feel their eyes glued to me, and I can sense a little smile coming back from them. Knowing that I made their day can be really rewarding.

Ever since the manager of my gym, LA Fitness, met me, he has called me Sunshine. He says that I brighten up the place with my smile, and then he makes a comment about the one little dimple I have on my right cheek. He never did know that going into the gym every day and seeing him made my day even better. It was his compliments that made me keep pressing forward. One guy at the gym would never look at me or smile. I decided that every time I went in and saw him, I would look him in the eye and smile. For a couple of months, he never smiled back, but now he smiles at me and we talk all the time. I can tell he's still sort of uncomfortable when I say anything about my height, but he shouldn't be. I understand it takes time, but I believe that if you spend too much time focusing on the fact that someone is "different," you lose someone who could have been your best friend.

I feel like I have a bond with children that is indescribable. We connect somehow. Maybe it's because there isn't much of a height difference or maybe because they trust me and think of me as one of their friends. Yes, kids stare a lot, but once I gain their trust, once they figure out that I'm like one of them, a wall breaks down and everything is good. A handful of them skip the staring and want to go straight to being my friend. It melts my heart each time I meet a precious little one like that. I work as a nanny for a family with two young and vibrant girls. I have many weekend babysitting jobs at their house where I get to play, feed, and love these young girls. The different conversations these girls and I share make my heart melt. It touches me when these girls will ask me for advice when we are in the middle of playing dress-up or at dinnertime. They ask questions about my life, and I feel like I'm having a conversation with girls my age, not girls who are five and seven years old.

A Hopeful Heart
There are lots of people who love me.
But one person's love is different.
She is a friend. A person who loves me.
She has a hopeful heart. She is my best friend.
She makes me who I am.

When one of the girls gave me this poem, I cried. Maybe I cried because I'm a very emotional person or maybe because at that moment I realized that these girls really looked up to me. I was humbled. My Instagram (@hulamadi) is full of pictures of my niece and nephews, and I have quite a few cousins who are all under the age of ten. I simply love children. Of all the wonderful things that come with being a little person, watching how children understand my differences and interact with me, is something special to me.

CHAPTER 12

My Greatest Fear

The LP life is not all sunshine and roses. While the good things definitely exceed the bad, I can't pretend that the bad things don't occur because I deal with them on a daily basis. I frequently get comments such as, "I have always wanted to be a little person," or "Your life must be so cool! I wish I knew what it was like to have your life." To those people, I simply just smile and say, "It is okay to wonder what my life may be like, but you should continue to live out yours, feeling blessed."

They should feel blessed that they don't have to walk in fear every time they go out in public, worrying that they could easily be physically picked up and harmed. Being only four foot one or as tall as a child, I often get scared thinking about how someone could pick me up and run away with me. If this were to happen, there is nothing I could do except kick and scream. I'm afraid as I pass certain people on the streets, thinking about the possibility of being kidnapped. It is one of my greatest fears.

I have heard devastating stories about how innocent victims are taken advantage of and never seen again, and I cannot imagine what I would do if I was in that situation. It is even scarier when men pull up next to my car or follow me just so they can talk to me.

I recall the time I was heading out to meet my mom and a man in a white suburban pulled right next to my car before I left the curbside. He told me I was cute and asked if I had a boyfriend. I told him I had a boyfriend, but I really didn't. I was just trying to get rid of him. He asked if I would ever want to cheat on him, and I said, "No, I'm way too young for you anyway." A few seconds passed, and I told him that I needed to leave, so he drove away. As he drove off, my mom came out to ask if I was ready to leave. She looked at me and asked what was wrong because I was shaking. I told her the story, and I realized why my parents always told me not to talk to strangers.

Right after that incident, my parents wisely gave me a little canister of pepper spray to carry in my hand while I am out for a run, or in my purse when I am out shopping. I always have it with me because safety comes first.

Little people fetishes just happen to be another fear of mine. It's something that's not often talked about. At any given second, I could be treated less as a human being and more as a powerless item to be won. There are people in this world who have a "sex bucket list," and little people often make it onto that list, as if we're some achievement to be crossed off. I've sadly had guys say to me, "Hey! I have never hooked up with a little person before." They are probably waiting for me to say, "Oh really, okay, I'll hook up with you!" Or many times I have gotten, "I've always had a fetish for girls that are like you." To those of you who want to switch lives, are you still interested?

Whenever I go to a nail salon, I leave feeling so pampered and loved. When I was younger, I often left with a slightly different feeling. The women working at the salon acted as I was bringing them good luck or something. They touch me, kiss me, and even give me money. When I was eight years old, I would often visit one particular nail salon with my mom. Every time I would go in, one of the employees would give me a little red Chinese envelope with a twenty dollar bill inside. This little red envelope is a gift usually given during holidays or special occasions. The red color of the envelope symbolizes good luck. Needless to say, I felt like it was a holiday every time I got my nails done at that salon.

CHAPTER 13

Perfection

What is perfect? According to the dictionary on my mac computer, perfect is defined as "having all the required or desirable elements, qualities, or characteristics; as good as it is possible to be, free from any flaw or defect in condition or quality; faultless. Precisely accurate; exact. Highly suitable for someone or something; exactly right. Perfect: Ideal, model, without fault, flawless, absolute, picture-book, beyond compare, without equal, second to none, too good to be true, incomparable." That's the definition of perfect.

Society puts a lot of pressure on girls and even boys in this world to think they have to dress or carry themselves a certain way. People start to believe they have to act like they have it all together or that they must look like a Victoria Secret or an Abercrombie model. Perfect isn't a size 0 or a size 13. It is not a number. Yes, it is important to be healthy, but one shouldn't feel like they have to be extremely skinny to be considered perfect. We seem to think that if we owned the newest pair of heels or a very expensive brand of purse then people would look at us as perfect, but perfect is way more than that.

God made us all different shapes and sizes, and He sees each of us as beautiful and perfect in our own way. We all have some body parts that we are grateful for. I'm grateful for my butt (yes, my butt), my smile, my small hands and small feet, and my one dimple on my right cheek. I would not trade any of these features for anybody else's. At the end of the day, I'm happy to have my father's thick hair and my mother's good looks with me at all times.

One thing that drives me crazy is people who spend so much time trying to make others believe they are perfect. Truth is, nobody's perfect. When we get all caught up thinking we are, we miss out on the world's joy because we are too busy being focused on ourselves. Most people are too focused on their own lives, their own worries, to even care. Stop trying to become perfect for others in the world and start working on your own definition of perfect for yourself.

To the outside world, I am different. I'm not tall, a model, or an athlete. To many, I am not normal, and they refuse to understand it. They can't settle for different. They need an explanation about why I don't look average. In my eyes, I know I'm different. So are you. No one is perfect, but we should always strive to be better human beings.

CHAPTER 14

College ... I Can Do This!

As I began college, I wanted to enter this new chapter in my life with my head held high and ready to educate others as well as be educated myself. My parents had been educating people about dwarfism from the very first day I was born. When I began to talk, I started doing it myself. I am going to be doing that for the rest of my life. I am happy to be given this opportunity to talk to people and share my story about how being a little person has altered my life and the lives of my family.

It wasn't easy accepting that my longtime friend, soul sister, and neighbor was going off to Colorado for school and it would no longer be possible to hang out with her whenever I wanted. We have been inseparable since we were young, and we do everything together. If someone were to ask me to name someone who knows everything about me, I would say Veronica. Veronica is my soul sister, and though we're not at all related, people swear that we are. We have been blessed to grow up four houses away from one another, so we've had no trouble finding time to hang out together. Throughout the years, our two families, along with the Wolfs, Sissons, and Goldbergs, have gotten together often to have BBQs, Fourth of July parties, concert in the park gatherings, and so much more. All the families have become super close. Now that we're all getting older and going down our separate roads, we know we will still be there for each other.

Loved growing up with these kids.

The first week of school was tough. I am amazed I survived. Well, I knew I would, but at the time it didn't seem possible. I came from a small private school where everything was taken care of for me. I tried my best in all my classes, and no one cut me too much slack. I received whatever accommodations I needed. In college, things were different. I had to figure out everything on my own, with no one holding my hand. It was a tough adjustment, to say the least.

My first week, I got dropped from two of my classes: English and Career and Life Planning. While my Career and Life planning professor let me back in (thank goodness!), my English professor did not. I was disappointed, but it was my fault. I should have been more responsible. All my life, I've told myself that everything happens for a reason. So after getting dropped from two classes, e-mailing, and going in to talk to my teachers, begging to get back in, I thought there had to be a reason for this, but I just didn't know what it was yet.

During that stressful week, I talked to a few friends from high school, and they all asked how I was enjoying college. As my friend Craig and I were texting back and forth, he asked, "Has anyone said anything rude to you about being a little person?" I stopped a second and realized how much I really loved that he asked me that. My friends from high school all heard my story when I spoke to the whole student body my senior year, so having my friends know that I was scared to start over was expected.

When Craig asked, I couldn't hold back a smile because no one had said anything rude to me at all. I thought that during the first week, I would get rude stuff said about me, but I was totally wrong. When I told Craig, he replied, "That's good! If they're not treating you right, you better tell me, and I'll come kick some butt." I stopped right then and thanked God for placing people like Craig in my life.

The second week was going along smoothly until Thursday night. I tried to get into another English class, and as I was walking through the double doors of the building, I saw a guy sitting on the floor, facing the doors. He pulled out his cell phone and took a picture of me. You might be wondering how I knew he took the picture. I know because the flash went off. He thought he was going to be slick, taking the picture and getting away with it without me knowing. He did get away with it, but I knew he took it. I posted about it on Facebook. By now you know I don't like people feeling sorry for me. After I posted, I received so much support from everyone I know. Most comments made me laugh, and most made me sit back and say, "You know what … yeah you're right."

"Did you look hot? Maybe he wanted to show you off."

"He probably just thought you were really cute and was too afraid to ask for your number."

"We go to the same school, so feel free to take a picture of him and then show me the picture. I'll take care of that stupid ass." Yes, I am truly thankful for all those comments. They meant a lot to me.

As the semester progressed, I fell in love with everyone whose path I crossed. College continues to be hard, but it is certainly exciting. I love the friendly people and how no one cares what other people think. I love when I am walking to a class and random people will say hi when they're passing by. I told my friend Jordan, who also goes to the same college, how nice everyone is and she said it's only because I'm a little person. Maybe that's the case, but maybe not. I don't want to believe that's the only reason everyone is so nice to me. If it is true, then I'm glad that they are nice and not rude. I love that I can make up my own schedule so I have Fridays off to do my own thing. I love that I am becoming independent and finding myself in the midst of everyone on campus. I love, more than anything, knowing I catch a person's attention.

In high school, I wanted to fit in and didn't like standing out one bit, but now, who cares! I am instantly going to stand out, so why not make the most of it and not care what others think. I love knowing that I caught a guy's attention. Who knows if the guy was looking because I was short—or just maybe he thought I was cute. Either way, he noticed me.

I am learning a lot about myself and how I have no one's standard to live up to but my own. I have kept so much inside that it started to take a toll on how I was feeling. There were things I never shared with anyone. When I got into a relationship, I soon found myself trying to climb right out of it again. Every obstacle I've conquered has taught me something. I love being independent and that it's up to me to make decisions for my life.

My sistaaa and I celebrating my 21st birthday together.

During the first semester, I was asked questions about dwarfism from a girl I met in math class. As I drove her to her car, we sat there and talked about relationships, judgment, children, etc. It was nice to talk like adults about what makes us who we are and what we want in life. I say that being a little person is a little bit of who I am, but as each day passes, I learn that I talk to people more about being a LP then I do about anything else.

CHAPTER 15

Surgery? Really?

Growing up, I never had serious health complications due to my dwarfism. I often suffered from headaches and sinus infections, but doctors gave me antibiotics and sent me back on my way. I struggled with nothing more than the average kid. On one occasion, I couldn't take the pain from my throbbing headaches, and I became aware of the fact that my balance was just getting worse. I knew it was time to see Dr. Yoshpe. Dr. Yoshpe is a board-certified otolaryngologist (ear, nose, and throat). She's helpful, informative, genuine, personable, attentive, and amazing. She is one of the best doctors I've had the pleasure of knowing. She is no stranger to my family. We have been going to her as long as I can remember, and it is always a treat to be able to see her.

At my first appointment with her, with my mom at my side, I told her what had been going on with my headaches. She had a CT scan taken of my head to see if a sinus infection was the root of all my pain. I knew deep down that there was something else causing these throbbing headaches and thought that maybe it had to do with my spine. I didn't allow myself to rush to conclusion about what may be wrong, so I waited for the results of the scan. Ten minutes later, Dr. Yoshpe walked into the room with the results and said that the only sinus infection she could see was below my eyes, in my upper cheeks.

She concluded that my headaches were not caused by a sinus infection. She worked with my mom and me to discover the root cause of the problem. We learned that the next step would be finding an orthopedic surgeon. Since I hadn't been to one since I was sixteen, my mom and I had no clue whom to go to who would still see me at my age. Dr. Yoshpe said that she would do some research and would contact us later. Shortly after that appointment, my mom got a phone call from Dr. Yoshpe herself and not one of her assistants. To me, that spoke volumes! At that moment, I knew I was on the road to finding answers.

Through Facebook, I connected with a little person friend who was in the process of undergoing surgery with a board-certified orthopedic surgeon, Dr. Kropf. I got his information from her and made an appointment to see him at Cedars-Sinai Medical Center in Los Angeles. After doing a lot of research on him, I learned that he has had over twenty years of experience specializing in treatment of cervical, thoracic, and lumbar disease and is an expert in disc arthroplasty, scoliosis, deformity, and fusion surgery, as well as many other things. I arrived at my appointment and he had me get an MRI and CT scan of my whole spine and neck. He had me share every little thing that had been hurting. When he brought up the scans on his computer, there was dead silence for a good two minutes. He looked at me and then looked back onto his computer screen. I knew by his facial expression that he saw something wrong. He looked back at me and said, "And you haven't seen anyone for this before?"

I quickly said, "No, what's wrong?" Silence again filled the air. I needed to have surgery.

On March 24th, the day after my mom's birthday, I was scheduled to have a relatively dangerous surgery. The operations to be performed were:

1. C1-C2 reduction of spondylolisthesis.
2. Posterior spinal fusion at C1-2, with bone morphogenetic protein, allograft bone, and Grafton putty.
3. Ventral lumbar laminectomy, spinal cord decompression, C1.
4. Placement of pedicle screw fixation.

My family and friends were nervous that I was undergoing this type of procedure, but I had faith that God had it all under control, and whatever happened that Monday morning was part of His great *big* plan. Though I did feel a little nervous the night before, I had an overwhelming sense of calm. I knew God was watching over my family in the waiting room and me while I was under anesthesia. Due to the many prayers I received, I felt a sense of peace. I was excited that there was a chance I could wake up every morning moving forward without a severe headache.

Early that Monday morning, I woke up, got dressed, and left with my parents to go to Cedars Sinai where Dr. Kropf and his cosurgeon, a neurologist, both who had both operated on many little people before, would operate on me. After checking into the hospital, I changed into a hospital gown and was hooked up to monitors. I started feeling anxious and a bit scared. Looking back, I realize I had no idea what was in store for me. I had no idea about the amount of pain I would experience or how long the whole recovery process would take.

The operation report told the step-by-step procedure of what took place in the operation room. I was placed in the supine position with my neck held in a neutral position while fiber-optic-type intubation was performed. Mayfield tongs were then applied and secured and locked into position. The doctors then turned me over on the table and secured my head. My neck was kept in a neutral and extended position. Next, the posterior neck and occiput were shaved. Draping was placed from approximately occiput all the way down to T4 to allow placement of their trans-articular screw fixation, C1–C2. Then they did the central incision from occiput down to approximately C3. The interspace between C1 and C2 was quite large, indicating a degree of previous instability. Many more things happened before the surgeons then packed bone graft into the C1–C2 graft with BMP as well as some allograft bone chips. Then they started to perform their reduction between C1–C2. Some drilling took place, and then the surgeons placed the appropriate-length screws across the C1–C2 articular surface. They fused the first two vertebrae immediately below my skull.

The hope is that the fusion will eliminate my headaches since my neck is now stable. I was finished with surgery and brought into my room, where I would eventually be reunited with my family. I don't remember much from when I woke up, but I knew my parents, grandparents, and my friend Frankie were right there when I woke up. It meant a whole lot to have them there by my side.

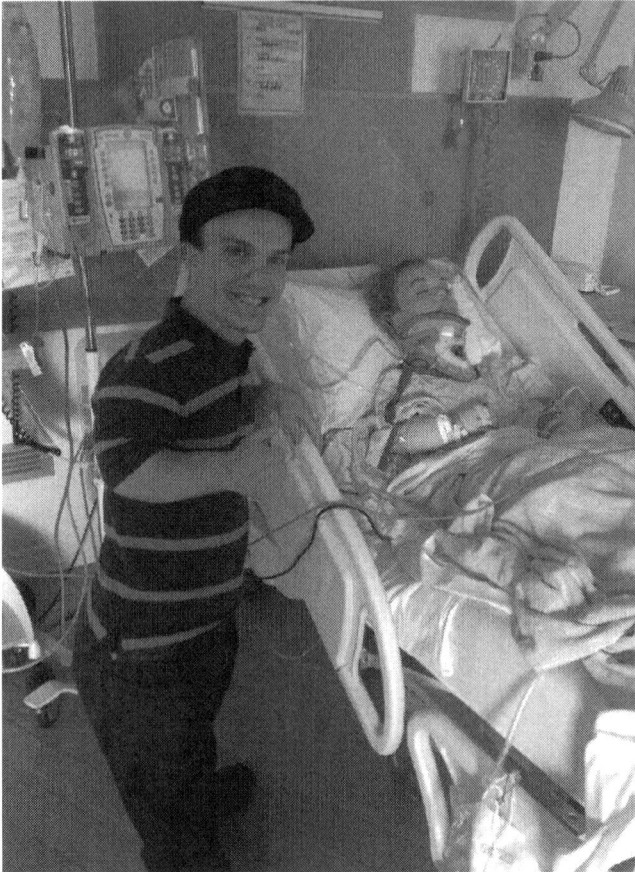

Just got out of Spine surgery

Two days after my surgery and the day I was supposed to leave the hospital and go back home, I collapsed in my mom's arms. It wasn't my first time fainting so she knew I would wake up soon, but

I eventually fainted again. Mom yelled for help, and nine nurses and one resident doctor ran in and laid me down on the floor. My mom heard the words, "She's having a seizure!" I came to find out I didn't have a seizure. The cause of my fainting was due to my neck brace being on too tight.

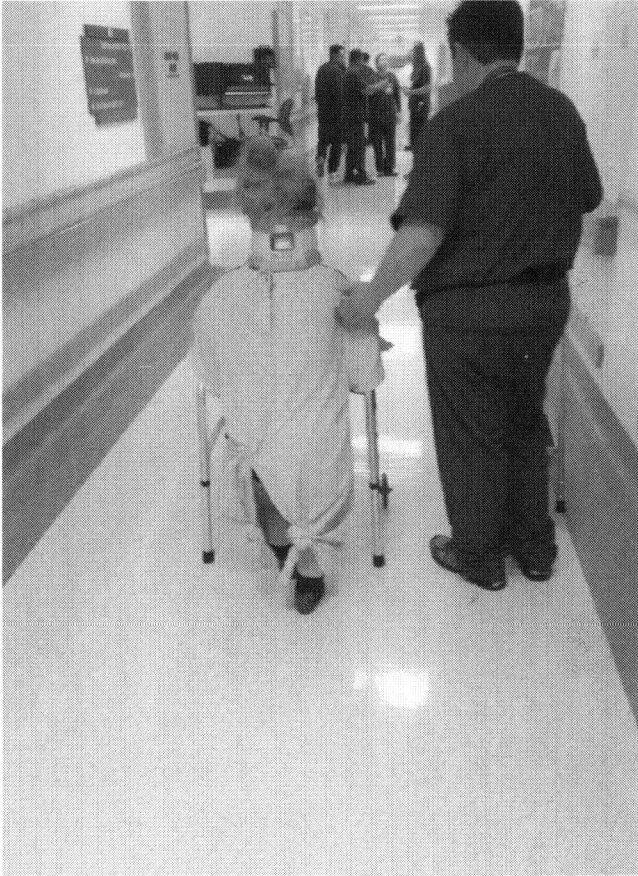

I was determined to walk so that I could go home.

The outcome of my surgery was phenomenal. The surgery went great, and I am still alive. I have experienced some pain and discomfort at times, but it was all worth it. I'm looking forward to no more doctor appointments for my misdiagnosis of "the sinus infection." For years I swallowed more pills then I would have liked and visited my family doctor too many times. Deep down, I knew those sinus infections were something a little more serious. I was in too much pain for far too long, and I don't wish what I went through on anyone.

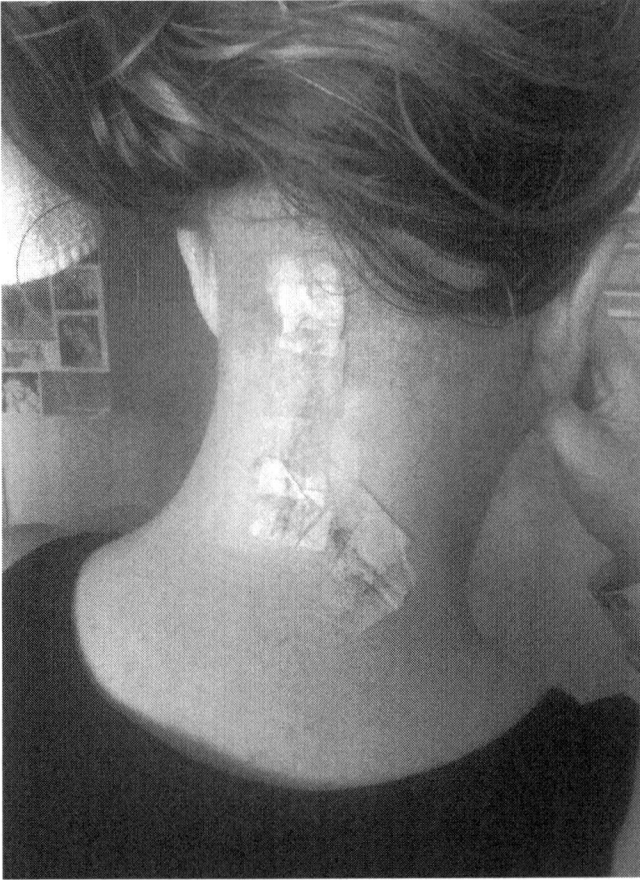

Everyone has a story and this scar will forever be apart of mine.

Before and after going into surgery, I received so much love and support from family, friends, and strangers from all over. During my recovery, I received cards, visits, text messages, and Facebook notifications wishing me fast healing. I feel completely humbled and a little blown away by all the love and support my parents and I received and continue to receive. Facebook notifications and text messages telling me to stay strong got me through the four days in the hospital and the painful recovery when I returned home.

I was very depressed at first, but today I am feeling good and can't wait to get back to driving and being independent. Showering, getting dressed, washing my face and hair, sitting up, and driving were all things I used to do by myself with no help at all. After surgery, I had to rely on others to help me. One of the many things I learned from this whole experience is to never take those simple things for granted. When I wanted to take a quick shower to wash my hair, I did it. When I wanted to go somewhere, I would jump in my car and go. I worked out at least five days a week at the gym for almost two hours at a time. After surgery, I couldn't take a shower when I wanted to and had to wait for my mom to help me. I'm still waiting for the okay to be able to start physical therapy to get some movement back in my neck. This surgery was just one of the many little speed bumps in my life. I know I'll soon be doing everything that I was able to do before.

CHAPTER 16

Prince Charming

$\mathcal{W}$e all want to be loved by someone other than our mom or dad; we want to be loved by a significant other. I see couples that walk past me on the streets every day, holding hands, and they all appear to be in love. I love my family, friends, the beach, God, life, smiling. I love all those things, but I sit and question why haven't I found *that guy* to love? Maybe I have, but I am too blind to see that he is simply the *one*.

Most girls dream of the perfect guy, the man she would call her Prince Charming, the man she'll marry and start a family of her own with. I dream about this man for me. What will he look like and will he be of average height or short stature? Where will I meet him? At school, in the gym, or online? A part of me dreams that perhaps I already know him, maybe only as a friend. I dream of what his personality will be like, and whether he'll get along with my family. Realistically I know perfect guys don't exist, but I also believe there's somebody out there that will be perfect for me.

Though I pray that Mr. Right will love, respect, and honor me. I also pray that I will love, respect, and honor him in return. We all have certain traits we look for in that special person, characteristics that will make us fall that much more in love with them. Most everyone in my life knows that I would love to find someone who's tall, dark, and handsome, but that's not everything I look for in a guy. I would love to find a man who is loyal, compassionate, confident, goal- and family-oriented, a man who brings out the best in others and has a sense of humor. I'm looking for a man who is outgoing and honest, one who is willing to try new things and take risks. A man who will appreciate and accept me for, well, me.

I want a man who's all those things, but most important, I want to be head-over-heels in love. I want to be with someone who doesn't ask me to be anything other than myself, someone who accepts me for me. I want someone I can laugh and cry with. I want someone strong enough to handle my tears. I want someone kind enough to know that while my story has made me who I am, some days it's all I can do to carry it. I want to trust and cherish him and wonder how I got so blessed. I want someone with his own story and journey and a person who knows that he has a purpose.

I want to love and be loved unconditionally. To me, unconditional love is when you deeply care about another person's happiness. To love and respect how they feel, and you have their best interest at heart and love them, flaws and all. By loving others, you look beyond their struggles, faults, and whatever pain and hardships that life could have brought them. "To love unconditionally is to love with absolutely no boundaries."

CHAPTER 17

I'm Here for a Reason

I always hear the saying, "You're here for a reason." Why am I here? Why was I the one hiding behind my mom's back when I was ten because I didn't want anyone to see me as different? Why couldn't it be someone else in my shoes and be me on the sidelines, laughing and pointing my finger? Maybe if it were you going through what we little people—or anyone else who may look different—go through, you would have a different perspective. You're you, and I am me, and life goes on. That is what I have learned.

Sometimes I just can't take it. I can't take all the eyes, the laughter, the questions, and the "Mommy, look at that girl!" Sometimes, I just want to leave wherever I am and go home because I have had enough for one day. I never leave, though because I feel like if I did, I would be considered a quitter. I think about all the little girls and boys out in the world fighting cancer or other health difficulties. You don't see them quitting. You see them fighting for their lives. They are all great examples for everyone who feels like they want to just give up. We should all walk the walk in fighting for our life and fighting for what we believe in. Keep pressing forward and keep looking to other people to inspire you. You can't do it alone. You need help. So get inspired by others or by situations that are placed in your path.

You have a beautiful life, so why give up? I felt like giving up many times, but hopefully I never will. My friends, family, and all the little kids I spend time with at the Children's Hospital, where I volunteer, inspire me to never, ever give up. Ask yourself, who inspires you?

All the eyes, pictures, and laughter get annoying after a while, but I know I can't change it. I am okay with being small and being different in someone else's eyes.

I love the way I am, even if it is difficult at times. I always say, "It's better me than you." I know that some people wouldn't be able to handle walking in my shoes for even a day. Some of my friends have told me that it would be hard for them to get adjusted. Life down here is harder than you think, but it will never stop me from having a smile on my face each and every day. If I came out of my mom's womb average, looking like I could grow and live an average life, then I wouldn't be the person I am today. I wouldn't act the way I act now, and I wouldn't be as mentally strong as I am now, either. Being created as a girl with dwarfism has made me a stronger person. Being a girl that gets treated differently has opened my eyes to see the world from a different perspective. God has a perfect reason behind why He made some people taller or shorter, or why he made a boy with brown hair and his sister a blonde. We are all children of God, so give each other a hand and minimize the staring, laughing, pointing, and the picture-taking of those who look different. Before you judge a person on their appearance, get to know them and have them share their story.

Despite having day-to-day trials, I am still a regular twenty-one-year-old woman. I cannot change my appearance, so I have to live my life in the body that God gave me. I'm an ordinary girl living an almost ordinary life.

We'll forever be life long friends. Veronica (VV), me, Emily and Vanessa.

Conclusion

veryone wishes they could have a crystal ball that tells their futures. I'm no different, and I wish that I could look into that ball and see what the future holds for me. I know that my future will be typical in some ways and unusual in others.

Currently, my dream is to be a speech pathologist and travel around the world, telling my story. We each have a story to tell, and it is your choice whether you want to go out in the world and share it. Telling your story to someone else can give them hope for their life. I hope my audiences will connect my life to their own, to the struggles they have to face and overcome. I know I won't be able to touch everyone in the room, but if I have an impact on just one person, that's fine. That's exactly what I went there to do. No matter what I go though, or where I go in life, I will not let my height get in the way.

I would love to have kids and a family of my own. If I gave birth to a little person, I would be worried about what they would have to deal with in life. As I am growing up and getting older, I see that I am treated differently each and every day. I would not want my child to have to go through what I have experienced, but I know if they did, it would just make them a stronger person.

As this book comes to an end, my life still keeps going strong. I am only twenty-one, so I have many more years to live. I have a lot more goals to attain. Thanks for joining me for the ride. My life isn't full of smooth, straight roads, but whose life really is? It comes with some bumps and turns; however, it's my life, and I'm going to live it to the fullest.

Thanks to my family and closest friends for helping me become the person I am. I love you all, and please, before you judge someone, stop and try to imagine yourself in his or her shoes.

ACKNOWLEDGMENTS

I want to thank God, my Lord and Savior, for giving me this beautiful life. Even though it is not always perfect, it is a life that I am truly blessed to live. Thank you for always watching over my family and me. It is you who created me and everyone else on this earth. I know we are all perfect in our own way.

Thank you to my amazing parents for bringing me into this world. I can't imagine what life would be like if I didn't have you to call Mom and Dad. I love you tons, and I want to thank you both for teaching me to be independent and not to rely on others. I have to do things myself.

Thanks to Rosemary Sissons, Karen Kain, Bonnie De Jong, Todd Civin, Erica Streelman, Jeff Westrup, Robin Robinson, Mrs. Garcia, Bill Garner, Nancy Winters, Ken and Marilyn Smith, and so many others for believing in me and for being mentors to me. If it was through encouraging me to write this book or just being my mentor through life and through high school, I am forever grateful.

I want to thank Brad, Mitch, and Dewey for being incredible brothers who have always been there to protect me. Even though we may not always get along, we are blood and we will always be siblings. Thanks to my beautiful, precious little niece and nephews, who remind me each and every day how beautiful life is. I see you three as if you were my own children, and I love you so incredibly much.

To my grandparents, who I have or have not met. Though my father's parents aren't physically watching my brothers and me grow up, I know his mom, dad, and stepmom are watching from up above. My mom's parents are divorced, but they are in our life physically, watching all of us reach our greatest potential. My amazing grandma, Ginger, has been by my side, encouraging me to get through school since I was very young. She has believed in me, and I appreciate everything that she has done for my whole family. She is #1 in my heart, and will always be. My Grandpa Jerry and his wife, Gloria, have always been there for me. They still think of me as a young girl. Though each year we would all like to stop the clock and become younger, all I have to do is go to their house, where I can always be that little girl that I sometimes still dream of being.

Aunt Cindy and Uncle Ralph have always been amazing godparents to me, and I can't thank them enough. Even though we are not related by blood, I love you just the same. I can always count on you to hang out for a few hours and as someone who will always come and pick me up. You have always been there for me, supporting me in all the important things that I have experienced, such as my graduations, birthdays, recitals, etc. I hope you both know how much I love and appreciate you!

A huge thanks to my incredible friends! Thanks for being there for me when I needed someone to talk to, and for giving me words of encouragement when I needed them the most. Thank you for accepting me and seeing me for who I really am. You have believed in me and helped me to believe that I can do anything. You have encouraged me to keep going when you saw me slowing down. I hope I make you all proud.

Last, but not least, I want to thank my doubters who have told me I couldn't do something and have never believed in me. Thank you! Thank you so much for giving me so much motivation to prove you wrong.

ABOUT THE AUTHOR

———————◆———————

*M*adison Mimi grew up in Southern California with her parents and three brothers. As the only little person in her family, Madison always knew her life would never be average. When she is not attending college classes to become a speech pathologist, Madison enjoys spending time with her family and friends, traveling, and surfing.

47587453R00067

Made in the USA
Lexington, KY
10 December 2015